Reflections of a Poet
I AM STILL

OLABISI DURODOLA
ALSO KNOWN AS
JOY WEAVER

Ordering Information:

Prime Seven Media
518 Landmann St.
Tomah City, WI 54660

Printed in the United States of America

Dedication

I thank, appreciate, adore and cherish the love of my GOD ordained wife, Oluwabusolami, who has through her love, made me a better man, a better steward of the living GOD and joyful father of children.

I thank the LORD OUR FATHER for the grace to be a loving Dad to two amazing sons, Olakintun and Iyanuoluwa.

Thank YOU EVERLASTING GOD for the grace to love YOU and enjoy being loved by YOU through JESUS CHRIST.

Table of Contents

About Faith

About Life

About Emotions

About Perceptions

About Romance

About Thoughts

About Tributes

About Views

About Faith

HAPPY NEW YEAR

May this year be your year of great joy and gladness of heart..
May your moments be priceless, colourful, and beautiful,
living a colourful and healthy life in CHRIST JESUS
May your seconds be impactful with good news and good success
May your hours be full and overflowing with perpetual joy
and gladness of heart
May your days be full of testimonies of the goodness of GOD
in the land of the living
May your nights be without regrets
but full of memories that make you laugh and rejoice
May your legacy be beyond your imagination
May we all celebrate many more times and seasons surrounded
by people we love and people who love us like JESUS.
I and all I love wish you the best, even more than words can express

DOES GOD EXIST

To be enraptured with the limited concepts pertaining
To the preambles of life
To be rectified within insignificant moments that waste away
Or engulfed by moments that are compelling, invigorating
Simplistic or complex based or eventually pertaining to ones view of
Knowledge or truth
Closed eyes trapped in bodies yonder simply wonder
Able-bodied individuals crushed or panged with pains
Chose not to accept or simply accept that hell is more fun
To be blind to sight is not a hindrance to ones soul
Yet it is by far safer as an excuse
Than to envision to realities of HIS divine presence
And still lose interest in the significance of perfect grace
To step into the questionable moments of time
And be at loss to the born again virtue
To acknowledge the evil ones lie
And be ignorant to the truth
That GOD does exist
Makes me that one soul
Blessed beyond the hindrances of life
To know that my GOD
Whose grace of CHRIST in my existence
Has indeed blessed the very essence of my being with
HIS love that I pray I share with you…
To take a leap of faith is my choice
To prefer the concept of finding out after death
That GOD exists is by far a better truth
Than the ignorance of the latter
I am human after all
Everyday is a choice…

HERE I AM TO PLEASE YOU

Here I am again Lord
Have I not said I miss you
I seat in the mist of strangers
Wondering were you are
I start my day refreshed in you
Yet at times the concept of who I am
Conflicts with the inspiration and truth revealed
By my companion and trusted counsellor
I yearn for you, just to please you
Yet I confess I am unaware
I have not the spirit of fear
But thy spirit of power, of love and of a sound mind
Thus I turn my eyes away from worthless things
And seek to be revived in your way
As I meditate upon thy words
My blessing and grace continue to enlarge
For I perceive I am like a tree
Planted by the rivers of water
I shall have joy in your strength oh lord
And I will continue to rejoice in your salvation
I stand firm on the solid ground of grace
That CHRIST has shown me
Yet Lord as I conquer all in CHRIST's name
As I yearn for the renewal of the spirit of my mind
Lord grant me the joy to hear your voice when you call me
For here I am to please you

LOOKING PAST

One perpetual moment is all it takes
one moment in time to look beyond…
beyond what i hear, feel, taste or see
to review every thing. Every moment
i said i will and didn't
i said i shall and couldn't
i must and can't, i will and
for the life of me… My bones froze,
my teeth tightened, my lips, my eyes,
My hands, my thoughts, my heart.
My body wouldn't burg.
All, everything pointed in one direction
for all hope was lost
i could sense myself plunging,
the weight of the world's waters crushing me slowly
but effectively. I guess my time was up,
no point praying for help,
"even GOD would look BEYOND my past"
i thought, yet my heart was pleading
Is that his hand of love I feel…?

BEFORE HIS LOVE DELIVERS ME

If I would, I should have
For with the fabrics of time
As of being here in this world
Full of life that isn't being lived right
Full of truth that has been modified to cover a lie
Full of lusts of the flesh that shatters the very fabrics
Of morality and decency.
Will I grow to be this individual harden to the ignorance of man
Or am I to forget the principles of GOD's unfailing love
Just because I want to fit in with the crowd…
My life is not really mine to live
Yet within every perpetual moment that transcends
The boundaries of time, I compromise on the truth
I live a lie and deny the grace of CHRIST
Just as it seems to please my worldly friends
While the friend who is truly mine I misrepresent
I defile my body everyday just to appear cool
Am I not indeed supposed to offer my Lord
My body as a living sacrifice; holy and acceptable to him
I am young, I still have time tomorrow
Yet I hear everyday of someone losing a loved one
But I am special I still have time to enjoy my youth
The night is young, the days are still many
Every perpetual moment in time that is mine
I shall live my way
Yet pain, suffering, sorrow, sickness,
The oppression of the devil continue to hound my very being
Is it my fault for compromising or must I be Holy and obedient before
Before CHRIST, in his love, delivers me

COULD I DO THE SAME

Is this a question?
Would I even allow myself to dignify it with an answer?
Everyday and every night, it seems to continue reverberating into
And perpetually penetrates the fabric of my being,
Could I love someone, a people whom I know emphatically hate me
Would I allow myself to justify love even though
He, she, them who torture me to the
To the very fabrics of my soul with all the evils that they are persuaded to imagine
I will not accept it, I cannot.
If it be that it is someone whom I love or an innocent child
For whom the prospects of tomorrow is formidably, as my heart and soul
Bear me witness…then a perpetual moment in time is to me justified to let go
To take my last breath and close my eye and move my essence to another
Another plain of existence…hum, I wonder
But I will not accept that one man could justify such love for me
Without me being personally convicted of the fact
They say HE is the son of GOD
Does that justify such love as described by those over zealous faithfully
Whom hide behind the banner of His name, shame, yes I said shame on you
hypocrites…
I don't believe them or could I…
Could I, if I was not blind, for my soul sees not…
Would I, if I were able to move a single cell of my body
As I lie in this vegetative state
Am I to be tortured with the bombardment of thoughts?
I may or may not have enough time
But death I pray…comes quickly
That my mind may be at rest
And my soul moved beyond into another state
Which would it be I wonder?
In Peace or turmoil…

FOR A TIME SUCH AS THIS

Simple realities, a GOD given…
Granted grace to witness
The sunrise. The birth of a new day
An encapsulating moment within the very fabrics of time
A quintessential moment to cherish
All that GOD has granted me the grace to love
I cherish the grace that my eyes
Even though closed, that I see the witness of CHRIST
I embrace the moments of GOD's perfection
When I see you smile at me just to enlighten and uplift my soul
I laugh when I reminisce of and over our perpetual moments in time
When I was weak, you were my strength
When I was strong, you kept me humble
When I was going to fast, you whispered to me
My child, slow down… I'm in control
When I felt insignificant and dull, your wisdom
Made me seem and appear exceptional in the sight of my fellowman
When I felt ashamed, your love covered me
When I was afraid, you kept me safe
When the foolishness of man, the devil fought me
You took my place and made me more than a conqueror
For such a time as this, that I may say and show
Before the sunset…
Before the very breath of life within me extinguishes
And I awake… to see you smiling and laughing with OUR FATHER
Can I, should I, I surely must declare…
How great and awesome your love and grace
Enhances my life…
Lord, accept my sacrifice of praise.

I CAN SEE

Yesterday, a day in my past, I awoke to a new dawn
A moment frozen within the boundaries
And comprehension of time as I know it
Yes I awoke and could not see,
I could not see that life had it's up and down
I could not bear witness to the pain and
Sorry that this world has offered me so often
I could not feel the burdens of stress,
Nor could I feel the oppression of satan and my enemies
The trials and tribulations that perpetually engulfs me with every breath I take
I was no longer within the very grasp of sin
Neither was sin in my nature evermore
CHRIST was no longer a perception of faith
Nor was he a practicality of the words I have read
Or heard from those who were his saint
No, CHRIST is…
How else can I express it…?
He who was, who is and is to come
Him I can see…
He is actually before me… standing with Our Father welcoming
Those ahead of me…
Those in front of me, wait a minute
Is it possible that CHRIST has finally come back?
Or have I arisen within the grace of resurrection
Wait a minute… where am I
Where am I…?
That I can see sure inexpressible grace of love and beauty before me

I STAND FIRM IN CHRIST

I stand firm in my faith
My faith to be all that CHRIST has made and chosen me to be
I stand firm in CHRIST'S will
His will to please and glorify the Almighty GOD
I stand firm within the path set before me
The true path of righteousness that only GOD has chosen for me
I stand renewed
Yes renewed in the spirit of my mind to do the will of Almighty GOD
I stand assured
Assured that with CHRIST all things are possible
I stand confident
Confident that all things work together for good for those who love GOD
I stand inspired and guaranteed
Inspired to say "if GOD be for us, who can stand against us"
I stand here to confirm
To confirm that "yet in all these things we are more than conquerors
through him who loved us"
I stand true to my confession
For with the heart one believes unto righteousness and with the mouth
confession is made unto salvation. Thus I confess with all the boldness and
courage within me that "Jesus CHRIST is Lord"
I stand alive,
Alive and willing to live on, only and only for CHRIST.
And as I continue to stand, I will hear, listen, obey and fulfil GOD's will
For I chose to flee from all youthful lusts but pursue righteousness, faith, love,
peace with those who call on the Lord GOD Almighty out of a pure heart
For I know that when I lay down and rest and close my eyes from this world
it is but for a moment
For CHRIST Jesus will lift up my soul onto his grace
And when I open the eyes of my soul
I will be standing before the
King of kings…

The LORD of Lords
The GOD above all other gods
The LORD of hosts
And I shall join the Holy Angels in worship singing
"Holy, Holy, Holy;
LORD GOD Almighty
Who was who is and is to come...?

SOMETIMES I FIND

Sometimes, most of the time...
Especially when I have being uninspired
Neglected, or wasted time in fruitless pursuits or dreams
I find that I hate the way GOD thinks...
Yes, I know GOD loves me and I really believe he knows best
What is best for me, why he has an essence that
May and does enhance the quality of my life
But I really hate the way he thinks
It really frustrates me... it really pisses me off
Here is a GOD, all-seeing, all knowing all able
With whom all impossible and impracticable perceptions and ideals
Can before the twinkle of an eyelid become
Manifested into the realities of man
I really feel like a fool even when I have prayed because I don't
I really don't know what to pray for anymore
Neither for myself nor for others...
Because even though I strive to be complacent with my limited faith
And get so ticked off with my insecurities about having faith
And working towards it, only to be made to feel irrelevant
Because my ideas and ideals don't have a place within the larger picture
And all my visions that have been instrumental to me building a foundation
To drive myself to success and prosperity seems to end up in the trash bin
Because GOD has a better plan...
And as I am not privilege to such info...
I am left in the dark to await the light to dawn on me
As I wonder fervently uncertain where and what my next move should be
Or if life in all the fabrics of wisdom holds any grace to
Better quantify or qualify the meaning of my further existence
I rang the phone but I feel He has put me on hold...
Sometimes I find that I just want to...
Need to hang up 'cause my faith ain't strong enough...

23

THE DIFFERENCE BETWEEN
A MIRACLE AND A MOMENT

Could light shine out of darkness?
Could hope be given to an ignorant mind?
Could choice be reflected as destiny?
Or could simplicity be beyond the quintessential ideal of love?
Why must I be astonished beyond words?
How can I not be able to comprehend or fathom?
Why there is someone as you in my life?
Night turns to daylight and I can breath,
Feel and taste the grace of you unimaginable, Indescribable and Holy moment.
Yes your perpetual moment in time as I seek first your
kingdom and righteousness.
I remain astonished and overwhelmed
at the miracle of you just being you Oh GOD…
Now I know the truth,
Yes the truth that the difference
Between a miracle and a perfect moment
Outside the boundaries of time.
Is that you…?
LORD GOD LOVE MOMENTS of MIRACLES
And JESUS wept…
Yes, I felt HIS tears cleanse me of my sins
LORD I thank you for the moment
That miraculous moment of grace
That showed me how much I am beloved
For as you said
"Father it is finished, into thine hands I commit my spirit"
GOD showed me HE and only HE has the power
The power to show that
I AM THAT I AM
Is GOD

THE VERY BEING INSIDE MY HEART

I just can't help myself…
It's almost impossible to envision a moment without you by my side
I awake to a new dawn, and the very first breathe of life
I take into my very being defines your essence
I open my eyes only to be bewildered by your essentially captivating
And enlightening beauty, your radiance awakens my very being to
The realisation that I am truly, richly and wonderfully blessed
To have you as my one and only love
Astonished by your beauty, with a dumbfounded gaze I try in vain to
Force myself off my bed, yet when you turn over and smile at me
I hold back the tears of joy… of unutterable and ineffable joy
That even a smile captured within the very fabrics of time
Renews my very being quintessentially with incomprehensible love
And I try to be the man only to realise that that isn't why I breath
I breath again just because your love fills me up to such depths
That all the oceans and all the seas, all the river and all the lakes,
Even if all the glaciers and ice made landscapes where to evaporate into clouds
All the clouds and all the rain drops from the very perpetual moment in time…
They venture to leave the boundaries of the heavenly clouds
To the very millisecond before the quantity of grace they contain
Frees the very earth of dryness… none can enhance the grace of love
That you…only you add to my very being.
You are the very being inside my heart
That astonishes me with such love
That even death wouldn't dear try to stop me…
It can't even get within the vicinity of hindering me from loving you
Who am I to be honoured with such essence of grace

'CAUSE I LOVE THE LORD

As times passes by
And experiences makes me…
Shapes me into a new being
I thank the LORD for uplifting my soul
Giving meaning and grace to my life
For HIS everlasting love
For HIS granted patience
With my existence
For all the moments HE has held me close
I must say how I feel
I must show how it feels
The time to say so is now
Cause tomorrow may not be
For you and me
The truth is here
CHRIST loves you and me
I have accepted it
I am living it
I am feeling HIM
Just 'cause I . . .
'Cause I love the LORD
I will enter HIS gates with thanksgiving
In my heart
I will enter HIS courts with praise
And I will dance with every breathe in me
For my soul delights in God's love
Thank you lord for loving me

TO BE EMBEDDED

To be renewed, to be refreshed
To be embedded in a grace that goes
Way, way beyond the mere comprehension of
Human mind and imagination
To start anew within confines that defines a better me
And enhances a better perception of you to me
I seek to find, I knock on doors hoping for the way home
OUR FATHER's kingdom
I wonder in hope for the days to come
Yet only one moment will it take to decide
My faith before heavens door
The book is open… I pray my name is written
I pray that the definitions of my moments
My perpetual moments in time will grant me the
Joy that goes beyond comprehension that is in CHRIST
For I hope that as I have remained and encouraged others
To be and remain embedded in HIS love and perfect peace
According to the order of Melchizedek
I will rejoice when I hear HIS voice
HIS own words that say "come unto me my beloved child".
When it shall be is just another moment away…

YOUR SINS ARE FORGIVEN YOU

I never ever thought someone
Could love me
I never ever trusted myself
Again to love someone new
I could never ever have anticipated that
Some being existed that
Could help me through
All the pains and sorrows in my life
And he said
Your sins are forgiven
Go, sin no more
Your faith has made you well
Go, sin no more
Your faith in me has seen you through
Come to me my beloved
Now I'm saved
And my soul's filled with joy
Now I'm blessed
And I can feel his love within me
Now I know there is hope
And it's there for you too
Just say please Lord
Lord JESUS forgive me
And he'll say
Come to me my beloved
Funny thing is…
When you trust him and obey his word
He also keeps his…

HERE I AM

As the choice is now
As grace commands that I be born again
As GOD's love demands that I repent
Repent from what
My choices are righteous yet my path is not HIS
Can I refuse to be human?
Can I renew the spirit of my mind?
As I turn away my eyes from worthless things
I confess the truth JESUS CHRIST is Lord
I realise that eyes has not seen nor ears heard
Nor has it been revealed to any man
The things GOD has prepared for
As I stand firm in CHRIST my chief cornerstone
I will not fail in my task
My grace to step out in faith for GOD is with me
As I prepare for tomorrow
I will finish my grace for today
For I know the truth
That I can do all things through CHRIST who strengthens me
As I wake up to exist within this chosen grace of time
I will declare that this is the day
The Lord has made
As I fight the good fight of faith
It is easy to see that HE that is in me
Is greater than he that is in the world
As the Lord is my light and my salvation
It is evident to see that I am more than a conqueror
Thus I declare that this is the day the Lord has made
Here I am Lord
Save me
Here I am Lord
Send me

HOW MUCH I CARE

Sometimes I really wonder
If anyone cares 'bout me
If anyone's really there
In everything I do
It seems there isn't a way through for me
I got problems above and around me
My peps trying to influence me
My family trying to force me
My life itself seems to show me constantly
That the bad always enjoy the times
So I wonder, does this GOD, if exists care for me
And he came down from his throne
In the form of a humble man
To express his compassion
And enrich us with his love
He enclosed us in his grace
Encompassing us with his love
Till the very, very, very last day
As he lay stretched in pain
And he called out to you and me
Saying this is how much I care
This is how much I love you
This is how much you mean to me
I will never, ever will I leave you
I will always be there
'Cause this is how much I care

As he called unto our father
Saying unto thee I come
That his love remains the same
He granted us the Holy Ghost
Giving us the power of his will
And before he departed into heavens
For us to await his return
He said
This is how much I care
This is how much I love you
This is how much you mean to me
I will never, ever will I leave you
I will always be there for you
Cause this is how much I care

About Life

A WASTE OF TIME

I am bored, don't you get it
I am really bored, I don't want to eat
I don't want to sleep, I cannot stand anymore TV
I just cannot take any more music
I am fed up of reading; I have had enough of trying
Knowing fully well that I am not, definitely not as smart as them
My soul has encouraged me for so long
My heart has carried me the distance
My mind has strained itself
Seriously beyond even my comprehension
Ambition and the ambitious, they come nowhere near
The talented and gifted souls of man
But what am I to do, I have being trying for so long
Praying and asking GOD for his grace
His grace of wisdom, understanding
The hope of insight and the reflection of knowledge
But all I do is try; I want so much to be the best
Not being proud or full of myself
Yet its totality is exhausting
I just pray that it is not, truly not a waste of time

AIDS

Who are you? Why are you such a plague to my people?
You indiscriminately accost and ravage my innocent people
Sentencing them to oppression that I have not sanctioned
As if poverty was not bad enough
You enrapture these innocent children whom I love so much
I cursed, yes I allowed my curse on those who choose not to listen to me
I made man for woman and woman for man
Yet I who gave the very essence of life the grace of my word
To exist I am considered a fool
While he who walks amongst them is to them wise
I cannot deny myself, for my word is faithful…
I will forgive all who seek my forgiveness
I will make whole those who acknowledge me
And I will destroy those who cause my people pain
Even the sting of death will not save them from my wrath
Yet for you my beloved, I feel as you feel
I hurt as you hurt, I know what stings he bring
Yet seek me while I may be found that I may heal you very being
And keep your soul safe within my temple
For the flesh will cease to exist
Thus your essence I will nurture for all eternity in my rest
Be not fooled I and AIDS do exist,
Yet before the very first perception of any of man's rudimentary
comprehension
Of the very fabrics of a perpetual moment in time
I have existed outside the fabrics of any quintessential moment in time
AIDS is nothing, My love has conquered

CAN I COVER MY FACE?

Life and liberties are an expression of your face
Expressions are compact, complex intricate gestures
That may or may not be a conscious
Aspect of our emotions
But when within the confines of a moment
A smile could be stored within the memories of another for life
A frown could become ingrained as an absolute dislike of another
Even way before he or she opens the ramifications of the tongue
A smirk, grin, sneer, a raised eyebrow and look of surprise we all know
The look of shock we all try hard to avoid
But what is life without the bewildered look of uncertainty
When life and it liberties force you to look to the heavens
As if to ask GOD a question, why...
Although I know all things work together for good...
*Can **I** cover my face now as*
The perpetually moments of my existence
*May imply **I** believe there is love... in HIS grace*

GOT TO DO

They say a man's got to do what a man's got to do
Who phrased this, who, for this quantum invocation
Has past, even further back in time
For today's world, challenges the very vigour
Of a man's existence, Man's inhumanity to man
The irrevocable damage of our hatred and pride
As we astonish even the child of the womb
How inconsiderate, selfish and hateful we are
We blame the item of hatred while we ignore
The growth of its seed in us, catastrophic…
The word that spells out ways we are lost
Thus the need to review the vivid prelude of our being
Man's catastrophes to man
The inhumanities of our souls as we ignore the teaching of love
Tell those ignorant ones that we are here
Now and ready to make a stand
We have got to do the renewals of our graces
For if our children are to love, we must first learn to stop hating
It is under GOD'S control, if we allow him to take control
The meaning of a man is defined by the ways of the man.

IF ONLY TODAY

If only today was yesterday
I would make right my wrongs
If only I had known, I would have lived
It differently
If only I had asked, he/she might have said yes
If only I had taken the risk like he did
I would have achieved even better than he
If only this, if only that
If only GOD would/could/will
Or allow me to do this I could
Or will become that
The excuses always start with an "if" in my life
I guess if I were to die now
I won't know what living is about
But now I ask myself
Am I not alive to change this 'if
Into 'this is'

IN THE HOPE OF TIME

In us we wish that there be grace
For in the mist of living in grace, the definition of man
The essences of the realities we live by are deemed great
When our compassion is our strength
Our love for our fellow man our weakness
For the realities we face today, is that we are blind
Blind to see that reality has being altered, what we see
Is but the illusion that evil and sin have masked upon us
The veil of misinformation, apprehension, compulsion, confrontation
Misdemeanours, mishap's, falls, and false fancies that cloud our minds
Yet in our moments of solitude, privacy, seclusion
Where we face our other half, in anticipation that we will conquer the
negativities of our minor existence, before our time is renewed
on the planes of existence
We know, and realise that, we need the love of CHRIST to see us through
We resist the need, for in the hope of time, we anticipate we are under grace
Yet, we know that death may be just around the corner, our limits exceeding
it Boundaries, we live in the hope of time; that GOD will not neglect us
For we still, still have time…
The fate we face, is that faith is of now, not a thing bounded by time
The next moment of life, may not be yours

IT IS YOUR FAULT

Yes, I *agree with them. It's your fault…*
it's your fault that the Sun is shining
today. It's your fault that I *am breathing*
this air fresh or otherwise soiled by the
ignorant disposition of mankind. It's your
fault that my wife had to go through
labour pains to give birth to our child
it's your fault that that hurricane came
and destroyed the fabrics of New Orleans.
It's your fault that so many people died
it's your fault that those who lived…
Suffered the cruelty and most despicable
attributes of man. It's your fault that
those bastards treated my child, my
daughter, my sister that way. Your fault
I *have no home to call my own. Your fault*
GOD that every single Bad thing has occurred
in my life. Now what you got to say 'bout
that you so called GOD. And HE said…

41

MEMBERS OF FATHERHOOD

Granted the pleasure was or wasn't great
Whatever the time may have been
Granted the timing was or wasn't anticipated
I your child have come
And, by GOD-given grace, I'm given
Your identity to bear
The definition and identification of you
Is written all over me
Even down to my very personality
Some of you have the courage
To teach me proudly to bear your good name
Some of you cowardly ignore
My existence till payday
Some of you shamefully dismiss me
For I'm a thorn from your past
The GOD who granted me grace
To be here today
Granted that I love you
Whichever way you've been part of my life

EVEN THOUGH I SEEKETH...

Of what worth is life, if I and my brothers,
Born of mother earth,
Fathered by our father
Nurtured through reality of
That which is good and that which is bad
Yet my brother and I have not brotherly love
Yet as we awake to the dawn of a new day
As soon as our hunger and thirst is no more
We earnestly seek our brothers' life
And as night approaches we seek our father
To thank him for the life and living
Our father, why hath we fickle
The word of your love, is it not the same
Yet…yet my brother seeketh my life
And I even I who ponder this melodrama, doeth the same
My heart, my soul, my mind,
My body help me love my brother,
Even though I seeketh his life

MY CREW

In life you need
As grace will allow you must
Even sometimes you try
But you can't give up your crew
To the peeps I call my crew
Friends that are tight and live
Mates that let reality set itself
On the graces we face
People I call on when I've got heat
Friends I hang with in my
Moments of joy and play
You call them brothers
You call them sisters
You call them family outside your family
You bring them home
'Cause they've let you into theirs
In life GOD blesses us with friends
If we ourselves are friendly
So this goes out to you all
Much love, much love

MY RULES, MY LIFE

It's my reality, based on the situations that
They, you, we, us and even myself
Make me follow
Watch yourself because come d-day
You only got yourself to blame
If you do it to him/her, the karma
Isn't going to let you forget what sorrow means
Aiming is the grace of ambition
Wishing without purpose flaws the principles of life
Max it up, for tomorrow is not certain
Yet if you mess it up, it is your fault
Life doesn't take responsibility of our situation
We do, for by grace our time to act is not
"I will cry, it's my right, I have to"
For the gift of true love is once in my lifetime
Problems, too much worry,
No matter how much I try on my own
I will always fail without GOD's help.
"By humility and the fear of the Lord"
So the word says, so I will live
I will dream of her, for it's my right
For my tomorrow with CHRIST assures me so.
My life, my rules
All I take from the word of GOD
For I know in it is my life

RENEWING MYSELF

Where have the days gone this winters dawn
Why are the nights in a rush to close the moments of the day?
I woke up in the new hoping to refresh and refine myself anew
The days of youthful ignorance have come and gone
The stage is set for the beginning of a new stage of my growth
I must admit, that the grace of CHRIST is my blessing
The love of GOD is my life
For when the moments began for me, I was a stranger in a new land
When the moments were hard for me, I was weak, and afraid
When the moments were full of joy and rejoicing,
I was loving and praising our Father in heaven
When I look back and remember the tears of my father as he said goodbye
I was indeed alone, yet when I began anew in this new but now familiar land
I must admit that GOD's love refreshed me true
His love granted my dream, my dream became reality
My fears a thing of the past, my present worries, in his shadow I abide
The time has come again for me to face another new day
The year's moments have been good and bad
Alas woeful, is the pace of man's inhumanity to man
But the breath of life is here, if it be I shall face the new day
I shall, I will renew myself...

THE DEBTS OF MAN

Isn't got a clue what to do next
It seems as if they all want a piece of me
They all want me naked
They all want me humiliated
A man needs this grace to renew himself
But they time me and limit my abilities
They threaten my sanctuary
They invade my mental well-being
I cannot take this anymore
Then I was out of a job
Then I was facing a situation
Far more antagonising than debts
Give me a little more than judgements
Allow me to at least try
Just be patient
I will pay; I know I owe it to you
Payday is just a few hours away
Mercy and grace is what I need
The pay check is almost here

UPON THE MEADOWS OF LIFE

For in the given grace of time
Upon the meadows of life
And the worries it brings
You see, you fall, you anticipate
Yet it never really is the way you think
Life itself is a grace, given to man
To accept beauty
But beauty in the heart of man is
Denied by the works of his hands
You are graced but you deny
You are loved but you prefer to hate
Loving is a GOD given gift
But the moments of our lives deny
Our souls the blessing that come with it
All, as far as grace has allowed
I realise is that GOD loves me
And I love and I'm trying to love him too

WHAT DO YOU DO

Actions pertaining from reactions
An understanding of a situation
As the situations themselves unfold
Either utter amazement and or incoherence
At the perplexity caused by this
Unforeseen or misunderstood complexity
Of the questions before me
The time line is short, the deadline is right before me
The count down of the seconds
The count down of the moments
They want this from me
But I can only do that
How do they expect me to finish this?
Unprecedented tasks, as if the money I get
Paid gives them the right
Actually, come to think of it
It does, oh GOD, I need help!
To panic will only make things worse
What do I do? What would you do?
The time is ticking, I need…
Yes, I need…

WHAT IS NORMAL OR ISN'T

The guess is yours
For your heart will tell you
The truth, your brain will help you think
But your body will eventually
Decide for you
Do this, do that
Why not, but why
It does, it doesn't
These are what I expect
This is what I get
Life only allows you chances
The opportunities will come and will go
If you waste time, time isn't going to wait
Ask yourself will I, or could I
Let GOD help…
And your tomorrow will be great
Trust in GOD is the key

WHAT SHALL I SAY

I have done it again,
And I know I promised not to
How could I have allowed myself?
I was warned, warned vigorously
I knew what I was doing. I saw it.
I saw it coming, yet…
Mum told me not to
Dad made me promise
My wife only forgave me because I promised
I even told my kids I was sorry,
That I will never do it again,
I remember the last time, how rotten I felt
This time feels a million times worse
I am cringing from within my soul
My body is self-suffocating me
It hurts how I could have done it again?
Oh GOD why did you let me
Why didn't you stop me?
What shall I say, what shall I do
This tape on my eyes has broken
My options, my choices, what must I do
Shall it be death, shall it be…
But wait, wait a moment there is another way
For if CHRIST is true then…

About Emotions

DON'T SHED A TEAR FOR ME

Don't shed a tear for me
Please understand that, hmm…
Ever since you broke my heart
I grew stronger
I grew more wiser,
I grew more…, just more better
Ever since you cheated on me
I have being enlighten
Ever since you killed me being
I have awoke
Ever since you stole my worth
My treasury of love has been overflowing
Ever since you made by eyes fill the ocean with tears
I have be lighter with no more sorrows
Ever since my body failed to sustain my heart
I have got to know my soul
Ever reaped love from my life
CHRIST has granted me the grace to trust in HIS
Be at peace my love, for loving you was wonderful
I pray whomever next HE grants you will love you more than i
But as for me, I have loved and love you still…
But you shall never be in my soul anymore
I am at peace putting my heart's greater treasure in GOD's love
Please don't shed a tear for me…
I am smiling more now, ready to love unconditionally again

55

LORD, I'M SORRY FOR BEING BITTER BUT I DID TRY

Lord, I'm sorry for being bitter but I did try
I tried to be faithful but my flaws are many
I tried to be trusting but was not trusted
I tried to hold on to hope but felt hopeless
I prayed for help but your helper was too far for me
I yearned to be obedient but time drained my strength
i tried to walk this narrow path of righteousness
but sin enticed me chaining my need and desires
as a man to another.
I am a sinner but i love CHRIST
I loved her unconditionally
She said she loved me but conditionally
Yet as i had been waiting, me and my sinful flesh
longing for your promise of a virtuous lady
only to be told after I had given my being to love her
that my faith was not right and my way of seeking
your kingdom through faith in CHRIST
was flawed by tradition.
But I thought faith and obedience was all that matter
Yet one can't be without the other...
She said she'll never marry me because of a uniform
Yet all in heaven are clothed in white...
sorry for being bitter LORD but I'm lost for words
to pray or praise. Please heal my broken heart

MY GREATEST PRIZE

Eyes have not seen or ears heard
the things OUR FATHER has spoken
nor has it been revealed to my heart
the plans and purpose of OUR FATHER
for giving me the grace, gift and responsibility of your love.
Loving you is one of my greatest testimonies
and I have a lot to testify about
You healed my broken heart
You restored me to HIS promised path
Your journey into my life
Your steadfastness by my side
Your tears that have watered the dying seed of our love
Your prayers that brings refreshing health to our seed of love
Your laughter that elevates me
Your presence that strengthens me
Your past, present that encourages me that our future together is blessed
I realise today that I am one of CHRIST'S mighty men..........
No matter the void that must be past
No matter the storm that must be withstood
No matter how lonely I feel on the battlefield against a world of enemies......
I will conquer ...
and remain victorious to the glory and honour of OUR FATHER
for I know my greatest prize is coming home to you my queen!

AT REST

Will a moment of bliss be forever?
Will the moments simply enhance itself when I am graced with your presence?
I awake to a new dawn to thank the Lord for His abundant love
Yet I say special thanks for the grace of you
And I asked Him have I awoken within a dream
Have I truly been next to such a vision of beauty?
With her enchanting smile…
Was she smiling at me…?
Yet when I awake from to be within these perpetual moments in time
I reminisce over tomorrow…
Has my rose just been in my imagination or will I…
When will I kiss, hold on, touch, feel and hear
The quintessential melodies of my lady Rose…
I pray GOD's mercy brings me her way soon
Before her next breath…
That I may share such grace
To keep my being at rest
Assured of love within the confines of another moment

SOMEONE I CANNOT LIVE WITHOUT

The age seems to creep but slowly
yet time in its reality has flown
the fact still reflects the moment
that my heart is still without her love
her name is… alas I know not
for in my dreams
she is my one and only, the lady I call
my essence, my queen, my love
for she is my soul mate in every way
for through every perpetual instance
and moment in time we share
for joy and sorrow, sadness and peace
every grace that life could grant
be it good or bad
has but bounded us souls in love together
for GOD has blessed our union
yet I see her in the arms of another
for she feels more comfortable with him
than with me. Profound as it may be
she is someone I cannot live without

DAMAGED WITH TIME

The feeling, is this, I am fed up
Fed up of not knowing where I stand
Fed up of the insecurities that time has bestowed on me
Fed up with them secluding me
Cornering me as if I were an endangered species
I have to make it but I have to wait
Why, why must I wait for another man?
Another being like me to determine my existence
I thought all power belonged to GOD
I had envisioned the notion of there being
Some higher being in charge of my minor existence
I need your help Lord, but here I am cowering
To and for the mercies of men that don't know or love you
Why must I feel or be made to feel inferior to the next man
Being told to leave the vicinity of their crowed graces
To discuss issues that I am unworthy to hear
I want to be the best but right now I feel I like
The dark dust that may not last another moment once
Noticed as unworthy to do the job
I feel damaged with time

I ONLY MET HER BELOVED

I only met her beloved
Yet how best can a stranger value someone else's mum
How else can you console a friend when He's, her's, their mum moves on
Moves on to her heavenly place in OUR FATHER's loving arms
You hope that to tell the world that Mrs Oyewusi was a
great lady would be sufficient
But that only lives emptiness
She was a pillar of strength, of hope and of faith
Yet they could question if GOD actually exists
But as she may have already told them
That she could see her LORD and SAVIOUR in the distance
Giving her peace before her journey
Her faith reassuring her beloved that she has gone home
Home to wait for us with CHRIST
Some may have met her and know how kind and wonderful a lady she was
Some may have called her mum even if didn't give them birth
But non know her worth except CHRIST and her beloved family
Mum is with GOD but the memories of how she loved continues to grow
Within the fabrics of the souls of her beloved
Can life go on without my wife?
Can life go on without my mum?
Can life go on when such love has been lost?
Her smiles reminds us that she has always said that
GOD IS GOOD
Even though her loss is more than we can bear
Our hope gives us peace
That we shall see you someday
In the loving arms and grace of OUR FATHER

We miss you…
We love you…
We love you mum
I call her mum even though I never met her
Simply because her beloved are my family too

ALL IT TAKES IF YOU WERE ME

All it takes if you were me
When you are stunned by such beauty
When she smiles and says hi...
is to open your heart and let her in
All it takes if you could wait is just to watch her
To watch the grace of her growth
The splendour of her facade
The succinctly simple ways of her love
The outburst the ravish you because of her passion
The foolishness that you feel when she leaves home
The weakness you feel when she is hurt
The pride you feel when she is full of joy
Never love her more than yourself
For you will cry more than you smile
But take it from me only a fool will want it any other way
For the moments of joy you once or may still have about her
Was worth it all, even if you know the truth about her love

DEAR TO MY HEART

Sometimes, somewhere, someplace
In life, within the lives we live
We view things differently,
We either accept or deny the fact we face
In some place, for each of our souls
There is someone close, someone dear
Somewhere within our perpetual moments of thought
Someone dear to us beyond the virtues of love
Sometimes I have to wonder how dear to my heart I can allow
Who could this person be, that wonders through my thoughts
Her essence within the air I breathe,
Her captivating virtue, stealing my heart away
My eyes beheld her once yet my soul…
My soul longest to behold her love again
As I hold her each moment dear to my heart

DO YOU STILL WANT ME?

Do you… I know it's not fair to ask
To seek the grace of your love, after all I have done
I do understand the level of pain I have caused you,
Saying these words of being repentant may not express the emotion of my
heart; nonetheless the ramifications of my existence as I seek your love
Implores that you here me, for I know that you are my perfection of love
Whenever I close my eyes to sleep, I find myself in the field
The field where great lovely memories grow nurtured by just the soil of love
I find myself sitting in our favourite spot, reminiscing over
the moments we shared
When you held me close to your bosom, as we reflect on the passions of love
Our perfect-moment in time, where every perpetual-flicker in our existence,
Was alive outside the walls of time. We fed on love; we lived on love
The birds sang our song; the lion curb curdled at our feet,
as if watching over us
For our love is worth preserving. I was about to kiss you again…
But my eyes of reality opened, and my heart ached with pain so vicious
I couldn't scream, couldn't cry, couldn't cringe… alas I could only stare
Stare at the walls of my life, as all the actions of my existence
were written anciently
I know I am a fool, to have let you out of my sight even but for a moment…
I know I can never repay you the damage I caused you soul…
I will remain on my knees in prayer, asking for God's forgiveness
I will remain alive as time if only in the feeble shell, in optimism, in hope
That just maybe, some day you will smile again, I love you my darling
You are my life, since I was one with you, from the very moment our eyes met
I have loved you, I really am sorry…
Do you still want me?

EVERY NIGHT

Sometimes the definition of loneliness
Comes from the soul the emptiness you feel
When you know you are missing
Something or someone
It makes you reminisce over the past
And forces you to dream about tomorrow
It sometimes even hurts
To the very core of your humanity
Making you a very vulnerable prey
Sometimes it makes you seek....
Seek ignorant comfort
Sometimes it forces out the devil in you
Making you do what you know is wrong
Mostly it allows you to seek the help
Of a higher being (I trust in GOD)
For I mostly pray that I find her soon
For I have loved her since my birth
I don't want to be lonely no more

FOR THE SAKE OF THEM

Some time ago, far into my past
The love and passion of these two
Made the grace of God's love for me
From her I came, by his strength I grew
They called me theirs, and I was their child
It was a great blessing to have the two
Yet them as I knew it, became each other
It hurt, it burned, and it made my blood boil
But at least there is no more screaming
The only shame is the one I knew
Is no more, But I know they love us,
Just that they can't stand each other
But for the sake of them, which indeed we are
Our love will always be for them.
Funny how things work out
I just hope and pray, that the love this blessing from GOD
That is truly from our hearts, mine and yours
Will last our lifetime, I do love you, wherever you are

HOW ELSE CAN I SAY?

How else can I say the words my soul longs for
and consistently seeks to express?

How else must I show that I long for her warmth in the

cold dark night of my being?

How else must I tell GOD that I can't take it anymore?

I can't wait any more for her to just look my way and smile.

I pray for courage everyday.

The courage to say to this lady I call by a name so

precious to my soul.

How else must I endure the pain of living another moment outside

her embraces?

Why must I stop myself from being refreshed by the pleasures of this
ignorant world?

Just because I long for perpetual moments of love

Why must I seek to love my wife as CHRIST loves the church?

Can a fool like me ever be so inclined?

My mum says call her, don't give up on love

Her mum says why haven't you called thy beloved

How long must I wait for her to
love me too…

HOW MUCH I CARE

Sometimes I really wonder
If anyone cares 'bout me
If anyone's really there
In everything I do
It seems there isn't a way through for me
I got problems above and around me
My peps trying to influence me
My family trying to force me
My life itself seems to show me constantly
That the bad always enjoy the times
So I wonder, does this GOD, if exists care for me
And he came down from his throne
In the form of a humble man
To express his compassion
And enrich us with his love
He enclosed us in his grace
Encompassing us with his love
Till the very, very, very last day
As he lay stretched in pain
And he called out to you and me
Saying this is how much I care
This is how much I love you
This is how much you mean to me
I will never, ever will I leave you
I will always be there
'Cause this is how much I care

As he called unto our father
Saying unto thee I come
That his love remains the same
He granted us the Holy Ghost
Giving us the power of his will
And before he departed into heavens
For us to await his return
He said
This is how much I care
This is how much I love you
This is how much you mean to me
I will never, ever will I leave you
I will always be there for you
Cause this is how much I care

I AM LONELY

I woke up this morning to realise my fate
Another year, another month, another day
Another morning, another hour, another minute,
Another second... another moment in my life without you in my life
I miss holding you my love, I miss kissing you my queen,
I fear GOD may have forgotten me in his busy schedule
Or may be I had you and let you get away...
That thought scares me, for I am so alone.
I dream of you every night, hoping that one of these days,
As grace will allow be it night or day,
I long for the perpetual moment in time
That our father and love will allow us
To breathe as one, body, soul, heart, mind...
Where are you my love?
Why are you not here with me?
My mind can't take it anymore
My soul is longing for your essence
I can't write this any more...

I NEED YOU

There are times that are moments.
Unforgettable instances encapsulated
Within the heart and soul of a man like me
For me life is only a grace, love is a blessing
I remember that very first day…
That perpetual moment in time
I was enchanted by your smile
And the beauty of your soul
My day lasted a lifetime…
I tried to focus on work yet I could only daydream
Replaying each moment in my mind's eye
How enriched my soul felt
When you smiled at me
Ain't felt the grasp of love as such before
Every grace I have had sharing a part of you
That I realise is a blessing from GOD
Has made me a better being, a full and fulfilled man
Loving and being in love with you
Is so enriching as I carry you within me every moment
I can't stop thinking about you
I find myself longing for you
Needing you within my every breath
That enhances my life
Hoping and praying that our love will overcome
And last till tomorrow
For I need you my queen
I need another moment to love you today

IN THE HOPE OF TIME

In us we wish that there be grace
For in the mist of living in grace, the definition of man
The essences of the realities we live by are seeded great
When our compassion is our strength
Our love for our fellow man our weakness
For the realities we face today, is that we are blind
Blind to see that reality has being altered, what we see
Is but the illusion that evil and sin have masked upon us
The veil of misinformation, apprehension, compulsion, confrontation
Misdemeanours, mishaps, falls, and false fancies that cloud our minds
Yet in our moments of solitude, privacy, seclusion
Where we face our other half, in anticipation that we will conquer the
negativities of our minor existence, before our time is renewed on the
planes of existence
We know, and realise that, we need the love of CHRIST to see us through
We resist the need, for in the hope of time, we anticipate we are under grace
Yet, we know that death may be just around the corner, our limits exceeding
its boundaries. We live in the hope of time; that GOD will not neglect us
For we still, still have time…
The fate we face is that faith is of now, not a thing bounded by time
The next moment of life, may not be yours

JUST TO SAY

I know now that I didn't give us a chance
I realise that I should I tried to understand what
Life, love and GOD's grace could bring through you
I guess I was scared, scared you where to young for me to love,
To cherish, to guide and be guided by…
Our words were clouded with emptiness
Our discussions were not enabling to, but fading into the night
My views contradicted yours and mine…
I was afraid that I was taking advantage
Advantage of a young, fast growing young essence
I was unable to see past what is…
As I have always been in search of perfection
Not realising that I was nowhere close to being perfect.
I guess what I am trying to say,
What I need to say, as a man, as a follow child of our father is
I am sorry…
For being a coward,
For being a fool,
For being afraid to let you in to my heart
For being unsure of the perfection of grace that you are
For letting you go the way I did…
I was angry at my uncertainties
Not at you, as such I had to let you go,
Praying that GOD will bless you a better love than mine.
I miss your smile; I miss your warmth,
I miss everything about you
Sorry I messed up.
I pray that this moment of my soul's regret will heal…
Any hurt I may have caused.

MUM AND DAD

Don't fall, no, do not drop.
Oh eyes please don't let me down
I can't I wouldn't
Let them see the pain in my heart
Tears are for babies
I needed to be a man now
Mum is crying
Dad is no longer
The young ones don't understand
I have to be strong
Mum needs me
What did he say again?
'Be strong son'
'You're the man now'
'You the man now'
How can I be?
Please heavenly father
Help me be this man
Oh dad
I miss you

NO MORE FRAGMENTS TO HEAL

Damn, what in GOD's name is going on,
How on earth could she
Why oh GOD, why?
What did I do wrong?
Haven't I tried?
Haven't I given up everything?
I opened up the purest side
Of my heart and soul
To love her
'Cause I felt this was her
I believed I had found
The perfect treasure all men
Were searching for
Damn, how, why did she
Choose him over me
I guess, now I know
Love's perfect wife
Is only a dream?
My soul is broken
My heart is smashed
No more fragments to bind
I pray GOD's love will heal
This putrid grain of pain within me.

OCEAN BLUE

Each moment that life gives me grace
and I see the ocean blue sky above
I reminisce over things that are
that could have been and may still be
then the drift quiets down and my thoughts
come back to the perfect moments
that life has grant me and you my darling
are and have been on top of that list
your smile to lighten up my day
your eyes to brighten up my soul
your touch to tingle me lovingly
your warmth, the wholeness of you
enriching my life with love
your laughter quenching all sorrows away
your sadness marking the true value
of living each perpetual moment for you.
My ocean blue love, each time you look up
day or night, remember I love you
my heart and soul miss you

SHE LEFT BEHIND

She represented everything I loved in a woman
She was the lasting piece of virtue
The blessing of grace that I appreciated dearly
Truly memories don't fade away when you love
It even lasts long if your love is truly from your
Heart and soul
I remember her smile, whenever she looked at me
I can still feel her kiss on my lips
Even though she isn't here
I find myself constantly reminiscing over her laughter
For it relieves the pain in my soul
I remember the sound of her voice
How it constantly reassured me that I was
Am in love with her
Even the content of her words help me be a better man
I constantly meditate over how she felt
Close to me, in me, one with my soul
Now I guess I will
I can only cherish the memories she left behind
She left me behind . . .

SHOULD I...

Am I asking or looking for this
This trouble that love brings
Should I say what I feel?
Should I open up my inner soul?
Or should I run and hide from you
Should I blank you out of my mind?
Or at least try
Should I call you, must I?
Should I say you bother me?
Should I tell the truth?
Of how great you make me feel
Or should I keep quiet
Hoping that tomorrow will
Solve my worries
Should I act the man and take charge
Or wait for you to make the first move
Should I be the pawn in this game of love?
Should I let you capture my crown?
The crown of my heart and soul
What should I do to win your love?
And express the sincerity of mine
Should I ask the question?
As to where I stand
Should I say I love you?

STRANGER IN MY LIFE

Intoxicatingly fooled and astonished,
Totally dumbfounded with my mouth ajar
Perplexed, yet truly intrigued,
Even my eyes gazed with disbelief
Griped by anxiety, terrified of the
Possibility of rejection, compile by hope to act
Grace with the breath of life
Inspired by the insanity, tempted by lust
My life has being redefined as I pray for courage
With each step I take the pounding
In my heart grows more intense
GOD, give me strength.
This stranger, this woman, this lady, this perfection of beauty, in my life
Has got me dumbfounded, flabbergasted, astounded, stunned
I can't feel my body, my words, my charm, and my will seems empty
Who is this stranger in my life? Everything about her
From her smile to the very way she walks
Defies everything about beauty I ever knew

THAT'S THE WAY IT GOES

Eventually what starts will finish
Realistically when things go wrong
Some day soon they will go right
Loneliness sometimes seems impossible to overcome
It's almost as though nobody notices you
Or just that, those who do only want one thing from you
Then you feel used, humiliated or belittled
You want to cry, eventually do
You feel dead inside and it shows on your face
The betrayal of trust and love
The hurt you feel, the pain that
Wants to kill your soul
But one day you get the courage to pray
And ask for God's true love
You close your eyes and feel at peace
When you awake to see the sunrise
It feels great. We all have ups and downs
That's just the way it goes.

THE FRUSTRATIONS OF LIFE

I was touched, yet angered
I was misunderstood yet troubled
I was made incompetent, yet I am able
The pressure keeps mounting up
My mind is being cascaded by the
Unmitigated ignorance of my fellow man
*She **is** this, He said that*
I can not think or ask what
Yet all in all only GOD knows the truth
Yet I am frustrated that...
That despite the much I do and little I ask for
None appreciates the little I need
My next choice is and could be...

THE IRONY

It is sad and utterly foolish
Yet we, yes you and me
Still do it over and over again
As for me I admit my irony
My 'if only's' are plenty
But my 'now I will', starts here
And only tomorrow will show
How I managed to change
"If only I had known"
To "on this day and during this moment in time"
I, by GOD's grace,
Saw my dream come true
The question is will you?

TIRED

How much more must I take
How much further should I go?
If time, in itself, has forgotten me
I haven't forgotten myself
I wake up every morning to a new day
Only to meet this so-called
Frustration, anger, malice and arrogance
Constantly looking for my trouble
Those who know me by now
Realise I have been patient
I have kept my cool
I have concealed my pain
I have soaked myself in the river
Just to let off some steam
I have taken up swimming, just to cool down
This rage within me
But now I am tired
Really, really totally tired....
I am going to bed

THE NIGHT BEFORE WE MET

I had, it seemed, always been, I felt
Some how my perception thrived on
The fact that I was alone
'Cause I feel, felt in a continuous context
That loneliness was a part of me
The night goes by so slowly
The wind blows and makes me shiver
The night-lights come alight
But the dark lonely night
Calls my name
I seek the comforts of ignorance
And receive only its sorrow
Feminine beauties, features seem to glare
But all was just emptiness
I earnestly sought daylight
And found time dragging it by
My incomplete shell arouse to seek
The pay of a new day
But instead I found you…

WHEN A MAN'S FED UP
WITH HIS WOMAN

She made me feel insignificant, turned me into a pet
She leeched off my sincerity, redefined me as a fool in love
I sought her warmth for so long, I prayed earnestly for her to be
I rejected the lust of my flesh, because I believed in the dream of our love
Everyday, every night, every moment time allowed, I tried to talk to her,
Just to know what I had done wrong, said wrong, acted wrongly upon.
If I was cheating I could understand that I deserved the cruelty,
If I were unfaithful, I would understand the words
'You reap what you sow'
I cried… I let my pride go and begged her on my knees
She didn't return my calls, even hung up on me…
GOD, please give me the strength to let her go,
For this is not the love I sought for
The pain needs to leave; I need to find another
True love is meant to be forever…
Its ups and downs are meant to bring us close
Our moment are supposed to be memorable
But right now I am fed up…
Tell me, what is a man to do when a man's fed up with his woman
All I sought was her love; all I did was to love her with all my heart…

WHAT CAN I DO

If you were me, and you knew the truth
The real truth about love, what love's really about?
What would you do?
Would you let her go when you find her?
Would you destroy a lifetime worth of joy
Just for a few minutes of pleasure
Would you mess up what took you over ten years to find
Just because some beautiful item winks at you
When you know fully well that her sorrows is forever
Would you seek to apologise later to your dream
Knowing fully well that you've forever damaged its perfection
Will you destroy your home?
For someone that will soon leave you condemned
How would you react to this?
This temptation is right before my eyes
Constantly telling me, have some, have as many as you want
It will be a moment well spent
But a lifetime of pain, sadness, loneliness, sorrow, anguish
Will I let the foolishness of me
Destroy what myself and I strove through eternity for?
This perpetual moment in time is my judgement day
I need to go home, I just need to…
My wife is waiting for me
For look at the odds, what else can I do?

WILL I SEE AGAIN

I awoke this morning, why I beg to question
For I realised as I took my first breath that I was blind
I was blind. Blinded by the truth I had long ignored
That reality that only HIS word expressed
I could not see myself beyond the beast I had become
How I had treated perfection with only a grain of salt
Watered with sand to feed the craving of my so-called flesh
My roar was rapacious. I went about looking for those ignorant ones to devour
Those mature girls whose depth of ignorance could only be enchanted by
Wit, smiles, cultivated words without meaning or worth as they keep
regurgitating from my lips as I feast on the desire for my ego
'He is tall, dark and handsome, so tantalisingly scrumptious'
I once heard one tell her friends as I walked into a club
'I heard her say she never had it so good before' she continued
Yet the very concept of love eludes me.
Will I ever find one who will hold me truly with love
as if I was taking my last breath
Will I ever find someone whose knowledge of GOD's love
will enrich the depth of my essence
With truth that no darkness can comprehend
Will I ever love someone, anyone who's worth
as a lady of virtue is worth dying to preserve
Will I ever feel her words touch the depth of my soul as I hear her say
she loves me?
Will I ever be healed by a smile even if the rain stops
Just to feel the radiance of her joy?
Will she ever look into my eyes and deliver my soul from the depths of hell
Will CHRIST ever say yes through her love for me?
For my soul to be saved to love her forevermore
Or have I broken her heart already
Was she amongst the hundreds that I have clawed my way though
Will I ever see again…?

WHY I DIDN'T CALL

I was thinking of how you were…
And how things are looking up for you…
I was going to call yesterday,
But I got home quite late.
In view of the moments that I have lost
The moments that I have not been there to look into your
Lovely eyes, the windows to your soul
I realise that I miss you,
I miss everything about not being able to hold
You close to my soul
To be there for you when you needed me
To be there to share in your laughter
To be there to encourage you in your times of sadness
If today were the only chance I would ever have
Saying, you are my queen,
Is but to express that you are
Beyond a special friend to me…
Hope you are feeling better.
Sorry I didn't call to say sweet dreams my queen
So I had to send this text as a picture of my soul…

About Perceptions

HOW I LOOK FROM YOUR EYES

I awoke today and doubted myself,
Unsure of how you would perceive me
I frantically wanted your approval but
I did not receive it, I doubted my very own
Thoughts, perception and dreams because of you
Yesterday I was so sure I could be the best
There was immense joy in my heart and soul.
My cloths seemed to match the form of my skin
My eyes glittering with joy
Because it felt like my dream was coming through
I could face it all, none, no one could stop my flow.
The shoes, the dress code, the summer specks
All matched and felt ready for me.
My sleep was spectacular, my slumber felt enlightening
The bath felt like I had cleansed my soul.
The smile on my face was so wide
And I was beyond ready,
Yet when I looked into your eyes
I saw myself and the way you saw me,
And I could but quiver
My knees quaked, as you reflect me
Lord please help me overcome my doubts
My next moment to the next will be if …

IF I WERE TO FIND HER

Yea, that is my question if I were
If I, Folahan, was to find this lady of grace and virtue
That GOD has chosen for me to love
To love and cherish the very essence of her presence
In my existence I would not hesitate to say or do what it takes
But alas the very concept eludes me, as I can't help but wonder
Did I have her in my grasp only to…
Allow my ignorance and fear of commitment to let her slip away
I can't help but question the stupidity that engulfs me
Whenever I realise that the lady I perceived to have the qualities
And radiance of grace that I long for in a woman that loves, fears GOD
Is only reflected in their quiet frank rejection of my concept of affection
Yet the irony is true, in retrospect, as I am often approached or
given the green light
By ladies whom I, in my quest only filter out of my equation of love within
the boundaries of husband and wife, a foolish ploy induced by my growth
From being in the womb to the moment of independence as
I have had to filter
Moments from my growth into this factorial figure of a man that fears GOD
Yet if I were… actually when I do meet her
I pray for GOD whom I love, to give me the courage to love his
beloved daughter
Just as CHRIST love the Church…

ANOTHER STILL MOMENT

As I review the possibilities
of my yesterdays, today, tomorrow…
I lay in wonder as to why
I face uncertainties in my life
I crouch in fear, I hide in shame
when I realise I have done wrong
wronged the ones I love
the only one that has ever loved me more
more than I can ever do
yet when he says
come to me my beloved,
and I will give you rest
my mind, my heart, my body, my soul
is mystified at yet another still moment
in GOD's love that calls me home
just another moment that might have not…
now is, by grace, in my reach

SEARCH

It maybe only once
Just once in this lifetime
When a moment may arise
To give you a chance
And the grace to define
Who you are, what you can be
Where you can go
How high you can climb
And the realisation of an impossible dream
That once maybe the only grace
Under GOD's love
That allows you to search
The memoirs of all the dreams
And aspirations you may have ever had
And if you chose the right one…
The realities of it will forever be
A blessing unto you and yours…
For you would have lived a thousand lifetimes
And go beyond yesterday's failures and worries
Thus search for what is yours…
Aspire to climb as high as you can dream
For with GOD all things are possible

PLEASE STOP SMILING

This isn't fair, it really isn't.
To watch the trickling showers of beauty as they
Catwalk down the stairs…Miss Italia
How can a sane man just pick one?
How can you be enriched with so much beauty?
Watching Bruce trying real hard not to smile…
Yea right! You see angels
walking downing the gates of heaven
and not wonder if they would say hello.
Romans… Italians… Could such beauty
exist within you walls.
How come her smile lightens up my soul?
How come her grace
makes me wish Michelangelo was still alive
to sculpt the her essence
How come her smile feels more enchanting
than the full moon in the clear reality of night?
Why is she smiling at me?
Please GOD, make her stop smiling.
Such quintessential beauty makes me feel
life has grace
Yet someone is missing…

SHE IS COMPREHENSIVELY

Standing but for a moment
Elegant in state, undeniably refined
I envision her grace
And remain perplexed by her radiance
How perfect are the works of GOD's hands
How immaculate is HIS craftsmanship?
For every single speck of dust HE used, HE broke the mould after you
where born
From afar, I remain enraptured with your captivating presence
I, gazing intently, I try…I try to look away
But the stillness of time
Holds me to ransom as each
As each perpetual moment in time spent
Being enriched by your beauty. Your beauty is
comprehensively enlightening
For your very smile uplifts my soul
I am alas but a man
Could I look at such beauty?
Such awesome grace and not
Thank GOD for the very grace of sight
For maybe, just maybe this is the very purpose of my existence
To praise the living GOD
For she is comprehensively
The essence of beauty defined.

SIMPLICITY AT ITS BEST

If a man be simple, if he be me
I will seek simply to be the best
For all I am, and all I seek to be
As simple as I may sound
Or as complex as it may turn out to be
It's simply the best
Thus with all simplicity I thus say,
If GOD grant me the grace to be
I will move on from I shall be
And seek to be simply the best.
Thus is the fuel for simplicity at its best.
As complex as the trail I climb may be
As demanding of my soul life requires of me.
As granted by faith…
As I have received what I asked
And found what I seek
I shall not falter till this door…
To me being the best I can be
It's opened, that I may come in…

SIMPLICITY IN THE WAYS OF THE HEART

If a man's heart were to be simple
If a man's words were to be true
If a man's eyes were to behold the simplicity of beauty
And comprehend the ramifications of love
If a man's thoughts was able to capture
And his body was able to choose the simple longings of his heart
This man would realise that he has finally out grown
All the lusts of the flesh, as true radiant beauty
As seen by a man in love with his lady
Comes from the virtue of this one woman who
In her character and ways of living
Will always enrich this man's soul
Beyond the physical measures and perceptions of
Worldly desires and needs.
And as such only GOD and his merciful grace
Will allow his choice of whom to love and this beloved
To unite within the perpetual moments of time

WHEN FAMILY NEED'S YOU

I sometimes wonder what our lives would be
Without the love, conflicts of our family
The pressures we go through, the pains we share
What could I but go when my brother needs me
How can I say no when my sister calls to me
My mother asks me what I have to do
My father shows me how I need to go about it
They are my reality when I go astray
Bringing me back to earth when I feel I could do no wrong
Helping and supporting me in desperate times
Rejoicing with me when life feels great
To GOD be the glory, for indeed he knew why
Why he graced me with the love of my mother
The fear and understanding of my father
The conflicting innuendoes of my brothers
The restful warmth and compassion of my sister
The soul mate I found in the lady I call my wife
The kindness and laughter of my son
The blessings of love that enriches my soul
Every time I see, hear, hold my daughter
Thus if my family needs me
To thee oh Lord I pray
Grant me the grace to be there for those I love
Yet even more so when it be my friends
Or an enemy in despair…

WORRIES

Did I sleep... did I venture to close my eye lids
Did I take a chance that I shall find some peace
Some peace and rest when I closed my eyes to sleep
These worries weighing on my shoulders,
Hunting my every thoughts,
constantly rampaging through my mind
My mind's eye constrained from dreams of what I could be
Yet I see myself that the brave and determined achieve greatly
Their history reiterating that there is hope.
It is madness and pain to hope and be patient
Yet in GOD's love I trust, thus I am assured...
That before my mind and body awakes...
The beauty of the sunrise will enlighten and brighten my soul
To face another perpetual moment as time goes by...

About Romance

AS I LOVE YOU SO

I got it bad; I earnestly face and admit the truth.
Each time I think of you
My heart opens, reveals and reminisces
Over an intriguing reality of love
My soul is encompassed with how it feels
The breath of life in me astounds me
As I vividly see my dream of tomorrow
Dreams of a lifetime of love
A passionate encounter,
A frame of youth, a painting of growth
An age of you and me
A perfect place to be for every perpetual moment in time
An appraisal of time lived in love and existence of today
You complete me in every way
From the simplicity of your quintessential smile,
To the complexity of venturing through the unknown moments
Of life with you and me as one
I know by, GOD's grace, the time has come
To ask you, as I love you so,
Will you…?

CAN SOMEONE LOVE YOU LIKE THAT

Can someone wakeup everyday of your life
With love in his heart for you
Can he, a man, with all the flaws men have
Wakeup wishing nothing more
Than to make your day full of joy and fulfilment
Could he look into your eyes every moment
You give him the grace to and you can honestly see
Your reflection in his soul
Can a man love a woman more than he loves himself
Can he complete you in words, actions and deeds
Can he be true to himself and open up his being to the love of the living GOD
And be worthy every breath you take loving him
Can a man willing to be chivalrous empty himself completely
Only for GOD to love you completely through him
Can a man's reflection of the love OUR FATHER has made for you
Spring you to life every morning...
Captivate the essence of every perpetual moment of you life
To the point that before you soul rests in peace
You can, you will, you shall...
Honestly and truly say
Thank you HOLY FATHER, for giving me
My husband to share your love with beyond what words can say
Nor actions express.
Can someone love you like that?
If you give me that chance to love and be loved by you
In CHRIST, yes you can...

AS THE SUNSETS

Life is but for a moment.
Moments that make or break the
Illusions of our realities.
Continents differ as the sun rises
Moments change as the sunsets.
Lifetimes pass by as our perpetual thoughts
Filters through the seconds that may lead …
Lead to years of bliss or of sorrow.
I'm but a fool, pondering if this is my life
Wondering if tomorrow would grant me one better.
As I can but exist in this moment
And pray that GOD's love leads us through
The good and bad things of living in this world
I pray that my soul will see the sunset with you
In my arms, comforting the longings of my existence.
Till then I look yonder, past the sunset for you, my lady.

A BLESSED MORNING
TO YOU MY LOVE

Hey sweetness,
Woke up this morning with you next to me
I realised you were still sleeping yet my soul found peace at staring at
you as you slept, it suddenly then dawned on me that I was not dreaming
I had finally found the hope of love that GOD had promised a fool like me
I watched you as you breathed softly, I smiled as I heard you toss and turned
I love the way you look fresh in the morning even though you are still asleep
I can't help to be fascinated and intrigued at how you body was perfectly made
to be more than I ever wanted in a black chocolate softly creamed lady
They say beauty is in the eye of the beholder,
I guess I am wiped. For when I look, I mean really look
At you I see GOD's handiwork all over you
My imagination however has a flaw, it can't imagine
how it feels being connected as one with you
For GOD gave us that grace as a treasure of his mystery
That pleasure blessed by GOD goes
beyond the limitations of lust or sexual immorality
For it starts and ends with love that
simply exists in the moments that take your breath away
Funny how when you were lying on my
shoulders I felt your heart beat synchronise with mine
and our hearts seemed to beat as one
Funny how when I watched you lay you head on the pillow
I could only pray that you were dreaming of me making love to you
Funny how when you turned the other way, I looked and seemed to be
mesmerised by the simplicity of your curves.
All I wanted was to paint you for the whole world to see
that Picasso had missed capturing this mastery of perfection
I could only wish I had Michael Angelo touch,
for I could not have carved an image
as close to how quintessentially astounding

I felt as I took in the joy of loving you
I always thought Toni Braxton was my kind of beauty until I met you
now I remain in GOD debts for I can never repay HIM enough
for having you in my life
for my dreams only stated hope, and I always awoke to faith
but every time I await for you to open you eyes and find me staring at you
I realise that you are a pure reflection of GOD's love for me
as I see HIM in your eyes when you finally wake up with a smile for me.
Only for you to say a blessing to my very being
"A BLESSED MORNING TO YOU MY LOVE"

I AM THE STRANGER

I awake you at night to make you
Wonder what may be. I allow you
to sleep in hope and anticipation of my
arrival or ... I commit you to things
that you know feels awkward but for me
You will do anything...
if I bid you live, you will live
if I wish you death, death obeys my scorn
if I choose you, you cannot deny me.
if reject you, I chose to, because I can
I am the one that decree your
joy and state of mind I am that one
that make the choices for you. My friends
whom I choose call me love, my enemies
call me hate, but I am that one that
is for I am not blind, for I see
through your mind into your heart
and filter through the flesh into
your soul. I choose whom I choose to love
Only GOD's grace denies me...

FOR THE DAY SHE WILL
SAY HELLO

Taking another stroll through life,
dreaming that this is the moment
the moment my existence will
forever be blessed by her essence
my eyes wide open yet I see her not
my mind pondering over and over again
in a quantum state of flux
mystified by the mere question
'where is she, my essence, my queen,
my true love'. Perplexed and confounded,
astounded as to why time, in its graces
has not rewards my prayers
I have thought my soul to be patient,
warned my body about the wrath of our father
Be still, and know that I am GOD,
my mind reacquaints me of his promise
yet the evidence seems far from near
I miss her so… I long for the day
the perfect perpetual moment in time
she says hello to me, myself and I

ITS NIGHT TIME

I have been a fool, a real fool
cause all I do is dream of virtue.
The price of a virtuous woman.
I have made my bed in wait for her
For GOD promised to help me find her
If and only if I don't ravage his
daughters. I sit on the seats of
patience as I watch my brothers play
the world of sculptured art-effects
of quintessentially and sumptuously
beautiful women. I grow in envy and
jealousy of what is and could have
been, if CHRIST was not in my life.
Teaching me how to love my neighbours
It's night time, and again I am
curled up in bed waiting for our
existence together as one
Some day, my love, our love will be
for dreams in CHRIST, do come true
I miss you my love, I really do…

BEAUTY

What is beauty?
Beauty is the delight that takes your breath away
Beauty is the marvel that renders its beholder in ore
Beauty is the absolute appreciation of God's masterpiece of creativity and
His ingenuity in the ultimate perfection of his works
But to a man is when within a perpetual moment
He loses all sense of control
And his entire existence goes num as he gazes at an essence of life
Both pure and real
Beauty to a lady, is when as she stares
She goes weak at the knees
As the goose bumps start to spring all over her body
And it feels astonishing
Beauty is perplexing
Beauty is excruciatingly delightful
Beauty in the eye of the beholder is mystifying
Beauty is when the fascination of a dream comes true
Beauty is immensely gratifying when looked upon
A picture of the best things in life
A gift forever to be appreciated, nurtured and treasured
To me, my love, you are the grace of beauty
For this is what awakens my being when I look at you

BY HER

Her smile was the first thing I noticed
For she opened up her soul with it
Hers were it, real, for they captivated me
Her beauty to me the beholder
Surpassed the likes I had ever come across
But her soul, her character
Her personality touch the very
Perfection of beauty
Her name sounded like a dream
And each time I meet her
My brain lost all interpretation
She, her, you
You are my dream of love
And in you, with you, by your side
I pray GOD, that loving you
Through each perpetual moment in time
Be the virtue of life
I seek and abide by

DREAMING BY MOONLIGHT

To sleep, to dream, to wish
To wish within my dreams that
These moments of loving you
My queen, will become my reality
Here I am holding close
Tight enough to hear your heart
Beating next to the rhythm of my soul
Here I love the essence of us
Us as one under the luminance of love
Each perpetual moment lifting us higher...
Higher and higher beyond our imaginations
Here I am lying next to you
Looking at your grace, the fullness of you
Thanking GOD for each moment with you
Admiring each trace of you
The perfections of the curve that makes and defines you
My minds eye picturing each intricate gesture
The way you breathe, the way you move
The ways you smile
Each articulate moment... priceless to my soul
I bless the grace of GOD's love within you
I bless the moments I remain within this state
But alas I fear that my eyes may close
I fight each moment to stay awake, to dream of you
For I know if my eyes should fail me
I may awake to the realities of life
Without you by my side

FOOLS IN LOVE

When a fool falls in love
He does not think
He does not know how to act
He does not know how to express his emotions
The fool rushes in always
Praying not to get burned
While his hands are over the flame
Experience teaches that love hurts
But time also heals all wounds
The fool in love knows this
Yet still opens up easily
And too fast
Hoping he has found his hidden treasure
The lady of virtue he was promised
The fool falls again and again
Then asks why he bothers
Alas he looks into her eyes
Mystified by the way it glows
He looks at her smile
And feels his heart beat
He grabs her and diligently kisses her lips
And he forgets what he was thinking of
Holds hear near, feels her passion and warmth
There and then he decides
Being a fool in love
Is all he wants to be

FROM YOUR FIRST SMILE

Alas, it seems like a dream
As I reminisce over and about
How you came into my life
The light of the sun presented
The dawn of a new day
The blue sky was clear and the breeze
Felt pure on my skin
I remembered to thank GOD
For the grace of life
And he blessed me and my soul with joy
You and your friend were walking by
But I had noticed your captivating smile
And perfect figure from afar
I felt the presence of your grace
And fell in love with your smile
The wholeness of you
Your beauty, I thank GOD,
Is defined by the worthiness of you
Even combined by your physical presence
Making you a perfection of GOD's grace
I linger at nights, and ponder during the day
Striving to understand
How this queen of virtue and love
From the moment of her first smile
Captured the heart of my kingdom
And the wholeness of me
Checkmate for life
Blessed am I

GLAD YOU AIN'T HURTING

When a Rose blossoms
Every soul is enlightened
For from such grace
Any soul feels blessed.
You are such a Rose
Yet when nature and its moments
Cause a slight change within you
We all fear what you may be…
My heart, my soul, my mind, my body
Thank the lord GOD for being with you
Now I realise the truth of the words
"If God brings you to it, He will bring you through it".
Funny how such a lovely Rose…
With all the desires of grace
Can be more than just a beautiful lady
Thus I'm glad you ain't hurting no more
May be tomorrow, I shall see you smile again.
Till then blossom, my lady…
Choose your colour and blossom…

I REALLY WANT TO

Striving and aiming that is all I have
Gunning for that post, that achievement
That distinguishes me from the rest
It's not that I'm proud or arrogant
It's just that I want to be the best
Someone special, talented in his own right
A genius to an extent, that of being or
Becoming a living legend
I don't and will not give up
But "the road seems hard, it is very hard"
I am scared I am not smart enough
Neither talented nor knowledgeable as them
But I earnestly seek the fame
To be one of the very best if I can't be best
Yet I never want to become a proud man
Just want to be the best man I can be
"By humility and the fear of the Lord"
Each passing moment I try to obey
Maybe later today I will be
This is the dream of my humble soul

IF A MOMENT

If a moment were to pass by
That holds the stillness of time,
It would have captured that perpetual moment
That I had you in my arms...
And asked... why didn't I kiss her
even though my heart knew why
my body was angry...
Angry that I didn't take advantage of the moment
Yet I guess my heart just needed, wanted our moment
to be a captured as a perfect moment in time.
Thus if time would allow,
and you grant me such grace
I await our first kiss...

IN MY VIEW, IT WOULD BE

Hello miss, could I call u miss
You see I have been regurgitating the words to say...
To such a grace as you...
Within myself from across the room...
From the very first moment
I was captivated by your enchanting smile
And the radiance of your beauty...
Forgive me for saying enchanting for indeed I was enchanted
I looked upon your grace and could only say...
Woo, GOD is good...
If I could make anything a perfect mystery...
It would be how I patiently crafted that smile on your face
For your smile could heal a dying soul
If I could intrigue any fool to ask a question
It would be for such a fool as me to ask...
Do you have a name worthy of such a quintessential grace as you?
If I could captivate the whole world to notice me
It would be for courage,
For I would live in each moment it takes to love you forever
If I could thank GOD for anything...
In my view, it would be for this moment...
Simply for the grace to look into your eyes...
For my very being is truly enriched as I exist in this perpetual moment
To say "to love you would be the greatest treasure of my heart..."
For if the Sun was to rise to awaken my soul
And grace were to allow a fool like me
If you were to be mine...
I would indeed live in the moments
of another day just to love you...

LOST FOR WORDS

You are just too good to be true
How can it be?
That a fool like me
Could find such love
Such grace, beauty and perfection
The most virtuous lady in existence
I believe CHRIST really loves me
For I owe it all to him
Who made us all?
Yet, patiently took time in perfecting you
My angel, my sweet heart, tenderness
The truth is
Each time you look into my eyes,
You smile at me
You hold my hands
You rest on my shoulders
I feel the tenderness of your kisses
I see the perfection of God's artwork
I taste the juices of your breasts
I feel the passionate motion of love
I hear your lingering sound of pleasure
I reminisce over all the above
Every fibre of my being,
My heart and soul,
To the very core of my existence
For each perpetual moment in time
That are and has been mine
I have been and still am
lost for words, my love...

THE WARMTH OF A TREASURE

A treasure is impossible to find
Yet to some, a very chosen few
A treasure is found after a lifetime search
To some a treasure is found after it was lost
While to the less fortunate and unprepared
A treasure is stumbled upon…
I found a GOD's treasure of love in you
Yet I never felt such mystery
For your warmth is a grace I thank GOD for
But your mystery is somewhat simplistic in nature
Yet a complexity of various realities
To love a queen implies honour
To be her husband is a grace from GOD
Who makes one king…
Your warmth oh queen is a blessing from GOD.
An intrigue and mystery I pray
I spend a lifetime loving. Never losing such a grace
And being fortunate enough as an unprepared man
To be crowned by GOD as your King…

MY BELATED VALENTINES

Simple words cannot express
the realities that GOD's loving grace has
in everyway blessed my life
Yet I remember the very first day
That exact moment
That just by saying hello
I met an angel of his
You are an angel of GOD's love to me
A friend that inspires
A friend that shares
A friend that understands
Sometimes I wonder what this life has for me
despite all its foes and trials
Despite all the worries and troubles
Sometimes I wonder what the point of living is
Then I remember your smile
and your words
And my soul feels at peace that
GOD's love is all I need
and his loving me through you
will always be a blessing to me
Happy belated Valentines Day, my lady

MY LADY MY LIFE MY WORLD

As I fall, as I live
As I will and truly do love you
As I have said I do
I pray GOD to help me love you
As grace has brought us together
As GOD's love is our joy
As today redefines
I am yours
And you are mine
As this moment is the building block
Of us, never again I and you
As yesterday announced that
Today is our day
As today we are born as soul mates
I thank GOD for blessing our tomorrow
For me this is the perfect moment
As I await the perfections of our moments to come
Oh Lord I love you
Baby thank you for saying I do
And as I look into your eyes
I hold my breadth
And dig deep into the foundation of my heart
And summon the words
My lady my life my world
I love you

REAR AND PRECIOUS

Rear and immensely precious
Is her love for it is her perfection.
Her value and her hold on the truths of life
Her dream
Only hurt and the aches of the heart
Will awaken her from the dream of
True and pure love
Her warmth is refreshing
For it touches the inner being
Her smile is perplexing for
It allows the beholder to perceive of the glow
She holds dear
Her walk is mystifying, for each step is that
Of a goddess
Her sound is captivating, for the whole world
Stands still, as it hears intensely
Every utterance of her lips
Much more is her value
For her virtue indeed
Is rear and precious

THE CONCEPT OF CHOICE

As I awoke to the graceful dawn of a new day
Sunshine trickling through the windows and curtains
As I awoke to a peaceful bliss in realisation of GOD's loving grace
My soul questioning me as to why I chose to let her go…
When she was as fresh as the air I breathe
As gentle as the warm sunshine that awakens and refreshes my being
As soft as the cushion I rest my mind on
As sensitive, even more so than the first moment my eyes
Opened to feel the intent and not just intensity of the sun
Why was the concept of choice made years ago hunting me now?
Was it just because she was now a woman?
Was it because I could see the lady of virtue I have been looking for since?
Maybe even before my first breath…
Was it because her eyes were still as clear as the full moon in a cloudless sky?
As I envision and continue to be enraptured, captivated, perplexed by her
very grace
Could a smile heal a soul hunted by a lonely life?
Could her words enrich my very essence with joy beyond words?
Could her soul bring me closer to loving and appreciating the grace of GOD?
Could her body and the sound of her essence move me closer to heavens door?
Could a choice made on a moral judgement…
Have been my biggest blunder?
I have searched all the heavens and earth for GOD to send my love to me
Could the concept of a choice transcend every perpetual moment in time?
And cause me pain that I may and did cause her…
As I let her go… her way.
For the moment I know not
Till I awake tomorrow at heavens door.

STRUGGLING TIDES OF MY HEART

In dreams flight, I climb above the skies
My soul's racing towards you
My every thought was of you
How I did hold on to the delicate grace of you
Being there when you need me
How I did look into your eyes,
The passions glowing from within me
How I did place my hands against your cheeks
As I elevate your lips towards mine
How I did place my arm around you
Drawing you closer with each breath I take
How I did press our chests together
As I affirm my lips on yours
Making the moments last a lifetime
How I did release your lips from mine
Opening my eyes as if for the very first time
How I did pour out the longings of my soul
When I finally conquer the struggling tides of my heart
And let time reflect my soul's desire to say...
For I do realise, my queen, my lady
My lady of essence...
That GOD's grace has helped me conquer ...
My fear of falling in love with you

THE MOMENT OF OUR MOMENTS

I miss the moment you looked into my eyes
the moment we shared the perfection of love
I miss the moments we held each other
I miss the dreams we've shared
I miss us as one, how we were
not individual complexities but
our mutual incredibility's and refined
simplicities. Loving you was, is and
Forever will be the perfection of my existence.
do you remember the day we met
the sparks and spackles that made
the moments of our moments, a blessing from
GOD. Words cannot express how lonely I am.
Actions will betray my soul, for I do...
the ocean blue sky, on this sunny day
is vaporising the pain from my soul
Making it rise fast to the heavens.
I pray my love, my essence, my queen
that you are loved well with our father

SHE COMPLETES ME

I won't allow myself
I can't allow my being
As I consider these offer the world
Presents and shoves at me
You see, she and I love each other
And as grace would allow,
Our love comes from GOD's essence
I must admit our problems
I must admit my needs
But consider this, after this moment finishes
You'll leave
And the time will linger on till the truth
Which is inevitable comes out
The consequences far outweighs
The moments of pleasure you offer
And no matter how often the pleasure may come
I'll only end up missing her even more
Her eyes, her lips, her smile, her voice
Her soul, her body next to mine
The very essence of her…
Sorry I'm such a fool but truly
I love my wife
For she completes me the way
GOD has made her soul love a fool like me…

THE TRAIN CARRIED ON

I and my soul are astounded,
revelling over the reason why
why she was in the next and not in mine
I have loved this lady all my life
her's was a major part of my heart
she had left without saying 'bye
years have mended my heart and soul
I was on the verge of moving on
I..., in arrogance thought I was over her
in the heat of the moment I stepped out
the thought of the instant was the very next step to take
yet my soul looked yonder, and our hearts skipped a beat,
a perfect moment in time yet the motion had
commenced and she was beyond my reach
instinct took over as I kissed my fingers
dreaming your lips will feel the impact
I hope the wind was on my side
for I prayed my kiss will reach you, my love

SEE YOU WHEN I SEE YOU

I awoke this morning with
The thought of you on my mind
How I have and do miss you so
We have and are facing times
Moments that challenges our will
Truth be told living with you
You in my life is where my blessing is
The joy I feel in the morning
When I sing so loud
When I make a fool out of myself
When the smile on my face seems
Permanently and affectionately glued to my face
It is all because of you
The joy comes from my soul
Vigorously shakes my heart into shape
Rampantly thrusting the melody of love
Throughout my body, refreshing my mind
With the blessings of love
The truth is, I have been alive 'cause of our love
But now that you've gone into eternity
I pray the love of our GOD bless you too
For since the images of you is all I have left
The memories of us to keep me going
I guess I'll see you when I see you
If grace will allow, as my moments go by

THE DAY YOU SAID I DO

For so long, for a very, very long time
I have been searching the world for you
I have been in agony, in pain, lonely
And immensely frustrated about the principles of love
True love, I said to myself she is worth the wait
True love, I said, will bring GOD's blessing to my life
True love, I hoped, will never hurt me
True love, oh true love, I asked, where art thou?
I had given up; I wasn't even bothering to take anymore notice
I had always known you were beautiful, never even thought you noticed me
I this fool of a man, longing for the dream of a virtuous lady
No I said, she isn't smiling at me,
It's the guy next to me, the really handsome
Really rich, the really popular guy next door...
The heavens opened and CHRIST poured his blessing on me
I looked up, I looked into your eyes, and I saw the truth
You said I do, said your love is real,
You said you'll forever be mine and I yours
The dream has finally come through,
She is finally here...
Be a man, please be a man, don't cry...
Why not, it's just my soul rejoicing...

THE GIRL I KISSED

I had thought it was she; finally my dream of her was here
I had accepted that I had found my dream
I had met the perfection of love
I kissed her softly, held her closely
Made her senses squeal with pleasure, as her desire grew for more
I was all but ready, I then realised the ramifications of my possible mistake
What it would mean in terms of shame, humiliation
Lose of face. I thought I had finally met her
I was and am ready for love
But alas what about the consequences of making love
Am I to allow the flaws in the imagination of man's foolishness?
Cloud my healthy fear of my GOD
She is, looks, and even feels beautiful
No I lie; she redefines this verb into a state of grace
The graces of the perfections of time spent in the perfection of her
Astonished, is the way she makes you feel when her lips meet yours
Perplexed is not even close to how her smile weakens you
Mystified is a close description of how her eyes confound you
Stupefied, stunned, flabbergasted, astounded, shocked
Aren't enough words, to describe how she makes
You feel when she says 'I love you'?
Bewildered, bemused, befuddled, taken aback, dazed, bedazzled
Reaffirm their meanings whenever love is made…
Woo, is this the girl I kissed.

THE GRACE OF LOVE

Days will come
Nights will go, for the sun has to shine
Moments to remember whatever they may be
True to each individuals' reality
Memories of good and bad
To be reflected upon
What won't break you
Will make you they say.
I say if grace be true and you
Be true to yourself.
Do good while you live and
The grace of love, which is the definition of GOD
Will be there when you call
For it is written
'Ask and you shall receive'
The reality of life is a GOD given grace
To love is the way to live

THE GRACE TO LOVE

To me, my one and only
You are a perfection of GOD's grace
My love, my sweetheart, my angel
For in everything you do
In everyway you do it
I not only see the effect you have
But feel the way others feel about you
Blessed are you amongst virtuous women
Indeed from the day I met you
You have being a fulfilment of GOD's love
To me and all others whom have met you
And for every perpetual moment in time
I have to spend with you
I will always thank GOD
For his loving grace
For I indeed, with every fibber of my being
Love you, my love
For you have given me and ours
The grace to love and the privilege to be loved

THE RHYTHM OF MY SOUL

Every time I feel good
Every time there is a smile in my face
Every time there's a glow shining from my soul
And it feels that GOD's immense love
And grace is upon my being
I realise that you have been around
Loving you has been and still is a blessing to my soul
You complete me in every way
And as I awake to face a new day
Through each and every moment time offers
I rely on the rhythm of love we share
'Cause my love, you bring rhythm to soul

THE RIGHT MAN

Here I am
Waiting on you to let me say hi
Struggling to find you
In this ocean of women
Longing earnestly to be yours
The part of you that you need
Want, dream of and pray
Will love you as truly
With all sincerity and decency
The kind of guy that listen to every
Utterance of your lips
The kind of person that will treat you right
He, your dream lover
That knows every inch of you body
Making your desires a perpetual reality
He who knows how and when to touch
Each spot on you
I have promised GOD that I'll love you
I have told myself that you are the one
The only one for me
I'm the quiet one over there
Scared to say hello

THE ROSE OF LOVE

Perfection in beauty,
Graced with the essence of love
Here's thinking of you
As the moments run by
For in each and every trace
Of what could be
You redefine, recreate and re-amplify
For every definition of you
Makes its mark of perfection
A thing that only one's presence
Will acknowledge as a true astonishment
For the time that I drew breath in your...
In your mesmerising presence
Is and remains fresh in my mind
This dumbfounded brother has to say
Lady, you got it all
For even your personality makes true the words
A thing of beauty, a perfect rose of love

THE WAY YOU WANT

Granted that I make lots of mistakes
Not forgetting my humanity
I, if you will allow
Come, appear, and stand in judgement
Of your conviction
Allowing myself to be judged
Crushed crumbled even trampled over
I have allowed and accepted the
Consequences of my yesterdays
Because I fear GOD
Because I need you
Because I need your love in my life
My apologies are endless
To the extent that I humble myself
And allow this degradation of my pride
I love the very essence of us
If this is the way you want
I accept, only please forgive me

TO HER

To her whom I love so truly and hold dearly close to my heart
To her who is my soul mate, yet nowhere near
To her whom I feel understands me more than I do
To her whom I love with every fibber of my being and she does too
To her, who completes me?
And brings love to every core of my soul
To this virtuous woman, my wife to be
I hope I find you before the wrong man does
For I know I am the better man
But you will probably think I'm boring
Until the other treats you bad
I love you and await your arrival in my life .
…My queen Oluwabusolami…
Now that you have arrived
To intrigue the reality of my being with your love
To make and redefine every quintessential moment of my
Essence, enhancing my conscientious existence,
The very core of my being with your love
I thank GOD for HIS and only HIS truth
That HE has poured into you
For when I look into your eyes
I see the reflection of GOD's love for me
For time, splits into moments that take my breath away
And I am left in awe, approbation, countless graces of joy
Simply because I think of you
I hold you tight even in my dreams
I feel awake and alive as a man when I hug you
I am left perplexed and astounded within your kingdom
Clouds cover my eyes as truth is revealed
When you call my name in a tone…

GOD hath not revealed any other woman but you
My world, my being and my grace is renewed
And time stands still…
Whenever you say
"I love you"

OLUWABUSOLAMI

Oluwabusolami is simply put…
the choice between excellence and extraordinary
For her presence is captivating, intriguing and refreshing
Her smile is healing, intoxicating and…
upon reflection a blessing from GOD
to whomever is within the grasp of her moments in time
Her laughter is soothing, amusing and fills ones heart
with pure joy…
I cannot imagine a world without her now…
Now she has graced my world with hope and faith
that to love GOD is an overwhelming reality
that can never be comprehended…
She has healed me with the sound of her voice,
and reminded me vehemently
that GOD is perfect in is creation of a virtuous woman…
I awoke with a smile on my face just because talking to her
Had made my perpetual moments in time last longer
With a resounding quality only she could have immersed me in…
She is a blessing to love and to cherish in the world
and a test of faith to whomever she chooses to love and call her own.
I cherish you…
for the moments you have seen GOD's love in me
and not the worldly garments I wear

TO THE LADY IN QUESTION

Hi there, my love, my sweet heart
Just thought I let you know
That dreams do come through,
The dream of love takes time
It lingers on, waiting for the right moment
However most of the time the power of lust
Deceives us into assuming we found the one
Sometimes the loneliness urges us so fast
We neglect the facts that are right before us
If you love someone and they don't love you
If you open up your soul, pouring
Out the love of your virtue
If you give all you have and it isn't coming back
This isn't love, not true love
For the fruits of true love are many
Joy, peace and rest of mind, compassion
The every moment thoughts of you
The knowing and remembering of the value of you
The need of you being there always…
I can feel your pain; I can feel your loneliness
I am too. I long to love you, I need your love…
But GOD will help us find each other
For we both need the right person to love.

TRAILING THE SUN

Thinking of how my soul would feel when the sun sets and I'm alone
I watch through the moments as the sun pulls the curtains over the sky
I watch as my mind is bedazzled by the
Intricacies of a single thought of you
I watch the clouds go by and I find myself wishing you were riding on one
I could feel my heart skip a bit, just because
I thought I saw you at a distance
Coming my way.
Why those the wind blow towards the north?
While I live in the south
Why are the mountains so high, hindering me from you?
Why are the oceans so wide and so deep?
Why is it so cold especially now...
Now that the heat of the moment
Has captivated my soul
Is the sun my friend, showing me the trail of you?
Or are all the elements of Mother Nature against me
For I have searched all my life
With every breath I take
With every fibre of my being
Through every perpetual moment I have lived
I have searched for the trail of your love,
My queen, my essence, my love.

WHAT IS A ROSE

A rose is the perfection of womanhood
The grace of her humanity
The definition of her character and personality
A reason why she herself doesn't and can't explain
Her attitudes and mystical fits
The rose of a lady touches and defines all her aspects
From her face, mesmerising
Her eyes, perplexing
Her lips, invigorating
Her smile, intoxicating
To her body, the curve mystifying
Her hips, ravishing
Her chest, bubbling with adventure
Her perfection, death defying
The motions of her critically damage the manner of a man
Never asks her to pick up unless she has you picked
For when her thorns pinch, you face the deadly realities of her being
For if she loves, you appreciate her thorns no matter how they sting
For if she leaves your love behind for another, the ponder shall never end
The rose, a perfect part of Mother Nature that even she would not
attempt to prune.

WHAT YOU ARE TO ME

If I were to close my eyes and make a wish
I, within this very moment, would wish that I were next to you
If I say how my heart feels every time I look into you eyes
Whenever I see your smile, even though you are miles away
My heart would show you the joys that you bring to my soul
If love could be any better, I know it is because of you
If I could hold you next to me, I would always tell you
That I love every moment with you
For you bring GOD's grace to my life
You are there to listen to my soul,
To enlighten me with simple rules of love
And complex actions of passion
You have taught me the values of a lady,
A woman of virtue.
To me, the meaning of you in my life
The worth of you in my life
You share your moments with me,
You redefine the realities of true love.
I am just a man living on the definition
The worth of your heart.

YET ANOTHER SUNRISE

Yet another sunrise without you in my arms
Yet another day without you by my side
Yet another moment without you next to my soul
If moments could last a lifetime
I wish I could always share my moments with you
Moments of every second that brakes into another day
Another day waking next to you
Laughing and smiling with you
If you were to wonder why I was staring
It's because I don't want to miss a moment of you
I don't want to miss the twinkle in your eyes
I don't want to miss any perpetual facial expressions
If you ever wonder why I hold on to you so long
It's because I want to remember every moment with you
How you feel next to me
How it feels euphoric when you
gently relax your lips tenderly entwined with my mine
How my body comes alive next to yours
Yet only GOD can tell if we shall ever be as one
Yet my soul thirsts for yours
Yet my moments without you are but years of want,
Need and longing for you, my queen…
Alas, the moments of this sunrise I share with you
Hoping, wishing, praying that soon,
I shall share it next to my beloved.

YOU THE ONE THAT I CALL

You are the one that I call my wife
You are the one that I call to my soul
You are the one that I thank the lord for
With every breath of my life
You are the one that I long to be near
Whose very smile keeps me full of life
You are the one that I call in my dreams
And with tears thank the lord are mine
You are the one that I call just to hear
To the sound of your voice just to make my day
You are the one whose smile I reminisce upon
As I face the challenges I have already won
You are the one that GOD sent my way
To guide my soul in ways that pleases HIM so
You are the one that I call our mother
As you grant me the grace to love our children
You are the one I call blessed
Every morning I awake to you smile
You are the one I call virtuous
As your essence is a fruitful blessing from GOD to me
You are the one I call my soul mate
As my soul longs to linger next to you
You are the one I call at the pinnacle of ecstasy
Just to hear you feel the same
You are the one I pray I die next to
Just to be able to say…
I thank GOD for every perpetual moment within time
I have loved you…

A TRUE REFLECTION

Could GOD be so kind, so kind to a fool like me
whose idea of love is but a fool's quest for love
that goes and endures beyond the boundaries of time?
Could GOD be pleased with me, pleased with possibly my faith in HIS SON
that HE would send you to be a blessing of HIS love for me?
I wonder if CHRIST is smiling every time I hold you in my arms.
For indeed if HE were, it would explain how at peace
I feel when I am in your warm embrace.
Or why the memory of your smile brings joy to my very being
Could GOD have spoken HIS word, finally beyond my expectations
for I have lingered, persevered in my sinful and foolish state
only to be forgiven when your love came my way
I wonder what tomorrow has in store for you and me
I used to be afraid, worried and unsure if life of faith.
Hope and love was worth
the inconvenience and discomforts I have felt
until I realised GOD had spoken HIS Word
and you became that reality for me.
The way you talk to me, moves my heart.
The way you pray for me, enlightens and enhances my soul.
I remember that I have something to fight and hope
for when you let me into your soul
I remember I have something to live for when you let me into your heart
I yearn for tomorrow when I become enraptured with your warmth
My mind remains intrigued by what grace lies ahead of
GOD's purpose for the both of us
If only I could stay faithful to HIM.
Could today be only a revelation of you
as a true reflection of GOD's love for me...?

About Thoughts

WHAT IT TAKES TO MAKE ME CRY

Is it true that I cry. Why shouldn't I cry
People cry when their loved ones pass away
Children cry when they get hurt. Women cry
when the one they love and have loved,
loves them no more. Men cry when it seems
that all is lost and not even GOD can help.
Funny how betrayal hits a man more than
truth. Yet what it takes to make me cry is
simplicity. The simplicity of sight. My eyes
cry these tears of joy for having loved a
virtuous lady whom I have never seen before.
I cry because having left this shell of mine
I truly saw how much of GOD's essence was
in every perpetual waking moment she ever
spent in my life. Is that not worth crying for.
To be alive and blind to see love
or not to be able, yet to have seen and having felt
its quintessential grace. Guess I chose...

A WASTE OF TIME

I am bored, don't you get it
I am really bored, I don't want to eat
I don't want to sleep, I cannot stand anymore TV
I just cannot take any more music
I am fed up of reading; I have had enough of trying
Knowing fully well that I am not, definitely not as smart as them
My soul has encouraged me for so long
My heart has carried me the distance
My mind has strained itself
Seriously beyond even my comprehension
Ambition and the ambitious, they come nowhere near
The talented and gifted souls of man
But what am I to do, I have being trying for so long
Praying and asking GOD for his grace
His grace of wisdom, understanding
The hope of insight and the reflection of knowledge
But all I do is try; I so much want to be the best
Not being proud or full of myself
Yet it's totality is exhausting
I just pray that it is not, truly not a waste of time

CLOSE YOUR EYES

Sometimes the mysteries of life have
And continue to grant mystifying intrigues
Of joy, of laughter, of sadness or of even pain and hurt
Yet when you sum up the great aspects of another being
Essence and grace within your perpetual moment of time
Her essence makes you smile
Her presence makes you joyful and blessed
Her grace captivates you into appreciating a masterpiece
Her words enchants you into feeling life
Her warmth mystifies you into compromise
Her handshake sends a tingle down your spin
Her smile perplexes you out of any thing contrary to joy
But the true defining moments of
such a blessing as her is her soul
Her soul refines the concept of GOD's beloved daughter
For to be within such a grace as her gives you a reason
To thank GOD for another grace of life, love and liberty.
Sometimes, just closing your eyes
You can see her in your dreams
Yet sleep was never your reason to dream

I REALLY WANT TO

Striving and aiming, that is all I have
Gunning for that post, that achievement
That distinguishes me from the rest
It's not that I'm proud or arrogant
It's just that I want to be the best
Someone special, talented in his own right
A genius to an extent, that of being or
Becoming a living legend
I don't and will not give up
But "the road seems hard, it is very hard"
I am scared I am not smart enough
Nor talented or knowledgeable as them
But I earnestly seek the fame
To be one of the very best if I can't be best
Yet I never want to become a proud man
Just want to be the best man I can be
"By humility and the fear of the Lord"
Each passing moment I try to obey
Maybe later today I will be
This is the dream of my humble soul

YESTERDAY, TODAY AND TOMORROW

I went through yesterday all alone
No where to go, no one to be with
Monday started off busy
Tuesday taught me not to hope for much
Wednesday filled in all the blanks for me
Thursday made me appreciate the good things in life
Friday gave me courage to fill alive
Saturday sorted out my weakness
Sunday, granted me love
And the appreciation of GOD's love
As night draws near, I again am mystified
For I only which I knew
What yesterday, today, and tomorrow
Had, has and will have in store
For a man like me

THOUGHTS OF THE MORNING

Will this be the day the blessing
Of her presence comes into my life?
Will I make a success of this issue
Before me?
Who can I call on to aid me?
How will I survive another day?
I need to get through this
I was warned, constantly
But now I know I messed up
Who can I call on now?
Or maybe the game will go our way
Will we, could we, how will I
Yesterday today tomorrow
Yesterday had its problems
Today brings its own graces
Tomorrow will be better
Than the memories and realities of yesterday
So as I awake, rushed and brushed with thoughts
I thank GOD for his love upon me

THE THOUGHTS OF TOMORROW

This and that seems to be
All that may and could have being
As your eyes demand, as your soul wonders
Was this heart now his, ever mine?
Although as I feel today, I know this moment
You are and always will be a part of me
A perfection in my path through life
Your smile, your lips, the wholeness of you
Defining beauty as a grace of GOD
Loving you feels and felt like a blessing
And each and every moment I think of you
I will always thank GOD for
The perpetual perfect moments
Of grace, love and joy we shared
With this thought of and for our
Tomorrows, I beseech you farewell

THE MANNER WE LIVE BY

"To be or not to be what"
If that question is still being asked
Being ancient is your crime
For now the question of today
That will aid our tomorrow
Needs to be
"Will it be, then when will it be"
For the positive mind will achieve the impossible
While the patient soul will conquer
And see what will be when
"Today will it be, then when will it be tomorrow" That is my question
For my manner of life, that which I live by
Is to see my dream of yesterday
Through all my struggles today
Become my reality tomorrow
Its time for being positive to come of age
By GOD's grace that's the manner we live by

THE ESSENCE OF TIME

I have, yes, indeed I have
I have pondered and thought
Yes thought day and night as I meditate
Over this question,
What is the essence of time?
Imagine the time it takes and took
To build up a life
Imagine the grace it took to have hope
Reflect over how it felt and still feels
As the moments of time go by slowly
As a turtle, crawling slowly indeed
Yet it flies by swiftly,
Faster than the wind blows
Sometimes it cheats us and deprives us
Yet sometimes it allows us to face
The reality that conquers evil
With the greatest weapon known to man
The grace of GOD's love
Even this time will only be.

THE AGES OF OLD

Sometimes you wonder
What it will be like when it comes
Sometimes you dread its arrival
If it comes what shall I do
How shall I feel?
Will I be all on my own?
Will they have left?
Who will be there for me?
Who will nurture me?
As I have become but like
A child comes of age
Will I miss my past?
Could I again long for a future?
As I see the balls roll by
Hoping and aiming is all I have
For when the time does come
Will CHRIST receive me?
Will my love for him see me through?
The greys on my head are many
Ages of time to claim me

STATE OF MIND

Ask yourself which are you
Find out, for indeed it defines who you are
There are those who think
And there are those who don't.
The world has revolved around this paradox
Since the dawn of man
These astonishing facts of life remain true
Man via man, the force of us.
The reality of man "is" to be
Yet in the moments within his breadths of life
He ponders over me, myself and I
Trying earnestly to figure out
What am I thinking?
How is my thinking going to better His existence?
Only GOD knows our thoughts of tomorrow
But in the "today's" that we live
We need to sort out our state of mind
For that is the only way our tomorrow will be great!
The moments wondering when, is far spent...

REPENTANT YOUTH

The total emancipation of time
Within the arrogance of youth
Rivalling the grace of peace
Struggling against the will of time
To know seems to be farfetched
To realise seems to only come with a
Frustrated and capitulating experience
Rise up and face the music is constantly
The sound that is being drummed and knocked
On the doors of our souls
But youthful pride and ignorant peers
In their pressuring ways influence me,
Us, we, to be what even hatred knows is pitiful
I have come to tell you now
That I want and need to grow up
For the streets only have death and pain to offer
I am tired of so called friends leading me to my death
I am frustrated at the failings that have complicated my life
I have looked for a way out but death seems to know my name
What if I were to die, surely it is and will be better than the life I am living
Yet as the moments pass by...
When I sit and remember all those
Awhile ago When he, she, they said...
Said that someone loves me more than I can ever love myself
Funny thing is through every moment I have lived
Through every perpetual moment I have taken a breath
And wondered from whence it came
I have been perplexed that GOD could love mankind so much...
HE could love me so much...

RAMIFICATIONS OF AN INDULGENT MIND

Again and again…
For this is what I see and feel
Do not re-address me for I am within…
Within the intricate climax that burns within
That implodes within the soul of a man
Do not indulge me, do not I beg of you
For every moment counts with me
Do not set my mind alight unless it is to intrigue
For what intrigues me, astonishes me,
For I'm faced day and night with issues
Of a blissful or yet mystifying nature
And my soul, my mind, my heart…
I within myself am forced to what…
What I acknowledge to be and not to be
The ramifications of an indulgent mind.

MY WILL, MY REASON WHY

Sometimes we wonder why
Sometimes we even ask
Sometimes we aren't bothered
But we know others are or just might be
The feelings differ, yet at times, are the same
One man does this and another doesn't
The feeling sometimes is as usual
Is there a GOD (I know there is)?
Why this, why that
The truth now seems to be
At the times of our personal achievements
We say proudly we did this and that
My will, my way isn't that
The reason why
I feel what I need to say
But I do what I don't

MY RULES, MY LIFE

It's my reality, based on the situations that
They, you, we, us and even myself
Make me follow
Watch yourself 'because come d-day
You only got yourself to blame
If you do it to him/her, the 'boomerang effect'
Isn't going to let you forget what sorrow means
Aiming is the grace of ambition
Wishing without purpose flaws the principles of life
Max it up, for tomorrow is not certain
Yet if you mess it up, it is your fault
Life doesn't take responsibility of our situation
We do, for by grace our time to act is not,
I will cry, it's my right, I have to
For the gift of true love is once in my lifetime
Problems, too much worry,
No matter how much I try on my own
I will always fail without GOD's help.
"By humility and the fear of the lord"
So the word says, so I will live
I will dream of her, for it's my right
For my tomorrow with CHRIST assures me so.
My life, my rules
All I take from the word of GOD
For I know it is my life

IN MY THOUGHTS

In my thoughts
However simple or complex they may be
However troubled and disarrayed my state of mind maybe
Or at peace the Lord may grant me be
I find a way and see the light
When feelings for you enrich my mind with thoughts
Thoughts of your smile,
Thoughts of your words,
Thoughts of you walking through my mind
As I see nothing else but a precious beauty
Filling me with peace and rest of mind
I thank GOD everyday, that he not only loves us
But he gave me the love of someone as real as you.

I AS ONE

The most invigorating, perplexing, astonishingly intoxicating,
Yet extremely joyful in effect and intriguing in life
That grace will allow,
Is the gift of love,
That is returned in its full quantity and feeling.
I love you my queen…
The complete build of me, myself and I
Depends on your love
I thank GOD for us being
I as one

About Tributes

TO DAD, MR D

Hi Dad. just thought to say hi once more…
I realise you are feeling much better now
Laughing and smiling at all GOD's joke…
You're probably making him laugh too
I missed out on saying goodbye earlier because I was…
'Cause I was not ready to accept you were going so soon
You told me you were waiting for me…
Sorry my game wasn't strong enough to bring us to see you earlier
When you were here to love
But I promise I'll tell her you taught me how to watch and pray
On bended knees…
I'll tell her how you had you flaws but was still man enough
To show loving-kindness to many
Maybe you loved life more than us
Maybe we just didn't get you
But I'll tell her I was proud to call you Mr. D, my dad
When my kids ask me of you…
I'll tell them you taught how to laugh and love GOD
Sorry I wasn't there to tell you I loved you in person once more
Just hope you knew that was true…
Say hi to GOD for me when you get the chance
And please stop telling jokes about how much I ate when I was young
A toast to you Mr D; See you when I see you dad…

LINGER A LITTLE WHILE LONGER

My eyes contemplate through and truly.
My soul ponders why and when.
My feet resent all attempt to
go and move.
I find myself entwined within the perplexing mysteries
Of the dawns early light.
Can I linger a little while longer?
Will GOD grant me the grace
Within my portion of these
perpetual moments of time...
To seek, to grow, to cherish or
understand why loving you my dear
lady seems quintessentially a
blessing from GOD.
As I start anew
at the grasp of my first breathe
As I open the eyes to my soul
Only to find you smiling at me...
I pray even before my body awakes
That today is another such day
That I may, in case for the last
linger a little while longer
In the warmth of my beloved lady

WALKING HOME

Guess my time is up. Guess that long walk
from my mother's womb has reached this
point. The point for me to define myself
as a man. The man GOD chose me to be.
Sorry, I didn't run mum, I realise you
might have wanted me to. But those whom i
love required me to be the man you raised
me to be. To stand up for truth, despite
the concept of hatred and evil that
surrounded me. As I remembered that even
though I walk through the valley of the
shadow of death, I feared no evil.
My soul was at peace, when I lost my grasp
of life. As I chased them away, CHRIST
called my soul back. Telling me my moment
was now, my purpose fulfilled. I kept my
head up and stood my ground, mum, for GOD
is with me. To those I love, just a word
to let you know, I'm walking home now…
Found myself a better place to call home

ANOTHER SPECIAL REMINDER

Moments may pass us by,
Times may distance family and friends
Yet when life grants us the grace to remember
We remember that those we love
Are right next to us
A birthday is that special moment
For us to appreciate the grace of their existence
That a bell rings in our hearts
To remind us that we hold someone dear
Someone truly valuable to us
Such is your day
A day for us all to tell you how special
You have been to us all.
Happy birthday Jacqui…
May GOD's love continue to be a blessing to you and yours

TO MY UNBORN CHILD

I see it in your mother's eyes
When she smiles at me
I feel it in your mother's grasp
When you go travelling within her grace
My hearing is redefined when I hear you
You the pleasure of our love
I beseech you come into our lives
I beg you love me
I, for I have loved you in anticipation
I have dreams of you and me
I day dream from sunrise to sunset
Your mother is truly charming
She loves you much more than me
So love her more than you love me
But love me too
I know we shall have fights of right and wrong
But even though I'll not always be right
But because I love you so
Grant me grace that I be right there
Always for you my child

TO MY MUM

To my source of life
In whom the very bones of my existence
Began to grow
She who accepted the seed that gave
Grace to my life
To this lady, who from my birth
Has been able to look into my eyes
And see the soul of the child
She carried in love
To this very lady who knows me better
Than I know myself
If time will allow, I'll shout it
If grace will allow, I'll show it
Though my soul and heart thus agree
If yesterday I forgot to tell you
If by chance one of us be not here tomorrow
I take this GOD granted grace
Today in this perpetual moment in time
To say how I truly feel
'I love you Mum, thanks for being mine'

THE JOY OF HAVING YOU IN...

Love is a funny thing with all the joys it brings
Sometimes it also is a frustrating emotion with some human traits
Yet all the struggles life has brought our way,
All have one perfect grace in common...
'GOD loves us' sometimes I forget that...
Yet it will forever remain true.
Today, this moment is by far
A blessing for me, us, our family
'Cause GOD OUR FATHER has granted another
Perfection of his love in our lives,
I awoke to the sound of a new dawn in my life
To receive the joyful news that you have arrived
You have arrived to reassure us
Of GOD's perfect grace in love
You have arrived to remove all doubts in our minds
That time has no meaning
You have arrived to enhance our faith
That the moments will keep passing by
That challenges will only come and go
But the joys and kindness of GOD is everlasting
Sometimes we forget, sometimes we ignore
Sometimes we even doubt...
But seeing your face, holding you close to my soul
Having your smile engraved into my soul, our souls
When the sparkles in your eyes comes with your smile
Assures me, us, our family that
You have been sent to fill the essence of our lives
With love, joy, peace and hope
Son, I thank and bless GOD for you
For the joy of having you in my life, our lives
Is the perfection of GOD's love and grace for
Someone like me...

SHE IS MY MOTHER

Who is this woman that makes?
Who is this woman that guides?
Who is this woman that builds?
Who is this woman that teaches?
Who is this woman that has been our grace?
Who is this woman that knows me more than any other?
Who is this woman that corrects us?
Who is this woman that encourages us?
Who is this woman that bites us?
Who is this woman that punishes us
Because she loves us?
Who is this woman that I love more than any other?
Who calls me?
And whatever mountain I must climb
Whatever ocean I must swim,
Whatever the weather may be
Whatever dangers I may have to face
Whatever it is I am doing
I will give up when she calls me
Who is she, who is this woman?
She is my mother.
I love you mum,
I bless GOD for the moment he placed me in you womb
And gave me the grace to call you Mother.

HOW A FATHER IS

Ten years passed by, lingered or well spent
Only GOD knows
How a father is towards his family
How a father is towards his wife
7 decades have passed
The time of rest and penitence has come
Yet all I see holding thou up are strangers
Mum has moved on, her home felt more
Blessed and at peace than him
He was not the man I knew
Yet I loved him even more so
For he had and continues to be a father to me
A loving man I continue to believe
Funny how the ink is already dry
How the sculpture is already perceived
Seems like we abandoned him to his wiles
Some even await his time to move on
He was a great man I had always thought,
believed and continue in faith to hold on to.
For he thought me how to pray and
How to trust in OUR GOD
Mum and dad may be apart
But dad is still dad
Even if age has finally left a mark
Or is it him reaping the seeds he had sown
Yet I know and believe GOD knows the truth
I can only hope he makes it
Home past Heaven door

181

ANOTHER BLACK MAN

He met an angel, a truer grace from GOD
I am still to meet
He lied about the joy in his life
A secret I hope he had the courage to have shared
Before she said 'I do'
She trusted in GOD
That this man was HIS blessing of love for her
I hear he has moved on
Even though she moved across
To the other side of the galaxy
Just to be with his black ass.
I am proud, to have this angel
This joy of a woman as my sister
He is lucky I guess,
For if our mother should know
Only GOD can deliver him
Even more so he should be grateful
For he married an angel
A lady of virtue whose only hope
For man was love that endured till the end
I guess he is just like me
Another black man foolish enough
To lose GOD blessing of love for him
I know one thing his true
He will 'be still'

MY LITTLE LADY

Born of grace, such grace from our loving father
You entered our lives, and granted us the blessings of your love
Just you being here to share our moments
Has renewed our faith and trust in GOD
For every reality with you is just amazing.
For every perpetual moment in time with you
Brings perfect joy to our souls.
Who am I, that GOD has blessed me so?
For whenever you smile you enlighten my soul with joy
For whenever you cry, you enrich my life with peace
For whenever you sleep, you nourish my being at rest
For whenever you awake, you bless me with moments of love
My little lady, my little angel, my little princess…
I thank GOD for every single moment I share with you
I pray that GOD's grace will teach me how to love you
I pray that GOD's mercy will always watch over you,
I pray that GOD's banner will always protect you
I pray that GOD's love will always guide you
For you see, my princess, I am only human
I can only love you with all that I AM
And I do love you my little lady.
Thank you for the love you
Bring into my being

MUM, I LOVE YOU

She who bore me and patiently raised me
She who knows every inch of me
For in her did I become me
She who says son I need your help
I need you here, right this moment
And I will walk across the face of the earth
Till I get to where she is
For because of her
Me, myself and I live and have learnt to live
"Son, be quiet, listen and learn"
"My son, treat her right for my sake"
"My son, read your Bible, it is the time"
"My son, you are wrong but I understand"
"Remember my son that when it's time
Do this and do that"
"Be a man, be a real man, that's all I want"
Her words ringing in my ears
For every situation that comes before me
Now that GOD has given me grace
To see her be the age of time
Now that I am the man she made me
I need to run home and tell her
To tell her what has be growing in my heart
Overflowing from my soul from my first moments.

CAN I CRY FOR MY MOTHERLAND

She held her baby tightly
While he or she fed from her breasts
Her others kids looking onward for mercy
Yet as she stood on the street begging for alms
A look of grief, sorrow and sadness
Covering her, overshadowing the blessings of being a mother
Clouding her with poverty and a look of shame
You must have been blind
Or simply heartless not to have noticed
Her pain, her heartache…
Sadness emanating from her soul
As she begged for alms
I wonder when she and her children had had a decent meal last
A meal that I probably would have thrown away
Simply 'cause it didn't taste nice
Oh what a spoilt child I am
My soul was in pain
As I felt helpless, fortunate, blessed
Yet saddened by the realisation that she was not alone
"GOD had not abandoned her" I consoled my being with
Can I cry for my motherland?
Should I even shed tears?
My nation is blessed
more than most I have been told
Yet her streets reflects the truth
about the living and the
concept of GOD's grace and mercy
As mum drove on by, not giving her a penny
I tried not to cry
For I realised we would never have enough
to help our motherland
to feed and love our mothers.

BLACK AMONGST
WITH THE ROMANS

I awoke to the dawn of a new day
Didn't try to make my bed,
Could not have time for prayer
Cause it might have meant I believed
Yet to feed my family
The woman who gave up
A life on the streets for me
Trying to avoid looking into
the eyes of my hungry kids
I will take care of you I had promised
As long as GOD takes care of us
I thought I handle being black
Black and living amongst the Romans
I will take every moment as a grace
And face the Romans…
I took my goods to face another day…
As the sun began to set
My belly rumbling
I saw some more customers basking in the sun
Enjoying a peaceful, joyful day
I could not help but wonder
why I ever crossed the seas in hope
Why I left my motherland
Yet it wasn't my skills that mattered
Nor was it my abilities to expand
Beyond the boundaries of my mind
Just can't grasp the truth
So I will press on in hope
Maybe tomorrow I will be blessed beyond this

About Views

WHY BOTHER

I am fed up of trying
I don't want to search anymore
I have tried to look carefully
I have tried to be a gentleman
But each time I come in sincerity
I get this cold and unnecessary shove
Constantly and repeatedly
I just want to be Goodman
One who fears and obeys GOD
But being patient is very
Hard, agonising, repetitively aggravating
Buoyantly frustrating, mostly a waste of time
It's so easy to play dimes, so easy to be bad
Unfaithful, exciting, funny, intriguing
Mesmerising and captivating
But ask yourself how bad must I be?
How badly must I treat you?
Before you realise that this isn't me
But as long as its how you want me
Why should I bother
Between getting some and not?
But I fear the lord GOD
THAT'S THE ONLY REASON WHY.

WHAT CAN I DO

If you were me, and you knew the truth
The real truth about love, what love's really about?
What would you do?
Would you let her go when you find her?
Would you destroy a lifetime worth of joy
Just for a few minutes of pleasure
Would you mess up what took you over ten years to find
Just because some beautiful item winks at you
When you know fully well that her sorrows is forever
Would you seek to apologise later to your dream
Knowing fully well that you've forever damaged its perfection
Will you destroy your home?
For someone that will soon leave you condemned
How would you react to this?
This temptation is right before my eyes
Constantly telling me, have some, have as many as you want
It will be a moment well spent
But a lifetime of pain, sadness, loneliness, sorrow, anguish
Will I let the foolishness of me?
Destroy what myself and I strove through eternity for
This perpetual moment in time is my judgement day
I need to go home, I just need to…
My wife is waiting for me
For look at the odds, what else can I do?

THE ISSUE IS US

Ever wonder why when we enter
It seems like they all keep quiet
Ever realised that the moment
You speak, they listen
Ever acknowledge that they whisper
As we walk by?
Ever found your self feeling watched?
Ever thought you had a funny smell
When you knew you vividly did not
So why every where you go
You draw attention to me?
You open your mouth, they, their ears
You speak; they note your every word
You act and your actions perplex them
You dress and they can't help but stare and admire
You smile and to them it's going to be a good day
You frown and they keep out of your way
Oh GOD, help my personality
For what they see is the issue of us,
You, Lord, living in me.

191

SEE YOU WHEN I SEE YOU

I awoke this morning with
The thought of you on my mind
How I have and do miss you so
We have and are facing times
Moments that challenges our will
Truth be told living with you
You in my life is where my blessing is
The joy I feel in the morning
When I sing so loud
When I make a fool out of myself
When the smile on my face seems
Permanently and affectionately glued to my face
It is all because of you
The joy comes from my soul
Vigorously shakes my heart into shape
Rampantly thrusting the melody of love
Throughout my body, refreshing my mind
With the blessings of love
I have truly being alive 'cause of our love
But now that you've gone into eternity
I pray the love of our GOD bless you too
For since the images of you is all I have left
The memories of us to keep me going
I guess I'll see you when I see you
If grace will allow, as my moments go by

MY STAND

Awake, with the wish
that life became a dream
furnished with everything
that will allow the very essence
of existing being a blessing
yet awake, I see with foresight
the reality of my dream becoming true
the odds are against me,
my tribulations are many
the trials are indeed heavy,
my weaknesses are draining my soul
Is it worth living? Why bother?
These debts are too much
no hope in sight
yet I will stand and make a stand
GOD loves me and I trust his love
I will achieve my dream tomorrow
but today, this moment I will make my stand

IN VIEW OF TODAY

This is my day,
For tomorrow for me, may very well never be
The lights may not shine
The rains may not fall
The lands may not stop quaking
The skies not stop thundering
The cries may continue, no joy in the horizon
But as long as love exists
For this moment is my moment
And I feel that…
And I am assured that
For GOD is my assurance
And I know …
This is my day

HOW DO YOU KNOW?

Funny isn't it
How can you know?
For the clock ticks whatever the situation
And your hands aren't big enough
To turn back the hands of time
How do you accept the reality you face?
Or how can you change the way
Your lives seems to complicate your existence
Why can't you determine your own tomorrow?
The answer lies in your today
This moment do you have the courage?
To pray for the Almighty's help
For that will always be the first step
He helps you know exactly how
It will be about everything

NOW THEY UNDERSTAND

Please do not infer I am to be…
for to be or not to be is not my essence
I will thunder… I will rain
I will strike fast with my lighten rod
Katrine was my cough… a tempest
Rita was my grace… a reminder
Ignore me more…
yes ignore me the more…
continue to pollute my freshness
continue to ignore my melting spot
continue to remove my groceries
continue your way, don't to say…
continue to think of me as an outcast
I will get up and move closer to the light
As my soul longs to cool down
It's time I let you realise…
Time I made you feel…
I just aren't called mother nature
for no reason.
For if our children are to love, we must first learn to stop hating
Its is under GOD'S control, if we allow him to take control
The meaning of a man is defined by the ways of the man.

TO BE LOST

It's hard I admit, to be stable within the confines of ignorance

It's perplexing I admit to be resourced within the limitations of truth

It's baffling within me to admit I can read…

But the depth to which I lack knowledge edges on stupidity

Oh, how agonising it feels to be lost…

There are moments that time grants us to be at our best

Yet the precincts of trivial matters

Beer, TV, Money, passion, desires…

Restricts me only to wait for death

I wonder if, maybe just if, I open my heart

And insult my own integrity

By seeking the knowledge of this so called CHRIST

Wonder how I'll feel tomorrow

I guess my view is all that matters…

I wonder…

Does this GOD really exist?

UNTIL THE CHILD IS BORN

Sweetness, my sweetness
May I call you mine…
May I call you the love of my life
May I call you the one and only love my heart beats for…
I have conceived a love for you in my heart, my body and soul agree
That loving you goes beyond being encapsulated with your radiant beauty,
'cause your beautiful.
That cherishing you everyday because I love you would be like
breathing to me
That longing to be with you, just to breath the air you breath would
be a blessing to my soul
That craving for you, just to hold you in my arms and make you smile and
laugh, would be a dream come through for me.
That making love to you would be the greatest day of my life
That loving you every moment of my life can only be surpassed by holding
our first born child in my arms to love with an even greater love…
Until this child is born, I will love you near and far away
But give me the chance, I beg you to love you more than I love myself
For seeing you everyday stuns me into silence…
Talking with you everyday makes me feel like GOD, who perfected you, is
smiling at me…
Because no one else in the world see you truly like I do.
I love you my sweetness, may I call you mine…

www.ingramcontent.com/pod-product-compliance
Lightning Source LLC
Chambersburg PA
CBHW021629120626
46545CB00002B/466